MW01680194

Relationships

Pondering Verse,
Book 1

by
Michael Kimery

PublishAmerica
Baltimore

© 2010 by Michael Kimery.
All rights reserved. No part of this book may be reproduced, stored in a retrieval system or transmitted in any form or by any means without the prior written permission of the publishers, except by a reviewer who may quote brief passages in a review to be printed in a newspaper, magazine or journal.

First printing

PublishAmerica has allowed this work to remain exactly as the author intended, verbatim, without editorial input.

ISBN: 978-1-4489-9630-8
PUBLISHED BY PUBLISHAMERICA, LLLP
www.publishamerica.com
Baltimore

Printed in the United States of America

"Relationship"
June 9th, 1992

Beginning with the attraction of first encounter,
Building upon the foundation of compassion and understanding,
Weathering the storms of misfortune and separation in distance,
Having the confidence in each other to trust, unquestioned.

The beauty of this relationship may be observed by all who have but the perception to feel.
There may be things that we would wish to have,
Possessions that would make life a little easier,
But the time lost, needed to obtain these goods, would not be worth all the gold in Fort Knox.

Precious is the time spent together,
Learning each others habits, idiosyncrasies, and preferences.
Making adjustments to accommodate each other,
And striving to make the other happier than they have ever been.

When life's time is spent,
The time spent apart is the only regret.
There may be rewards to follow this earthly coil of flesh and bone,
But the rewards of sharing your life with a spouse on earth seems to me the essence of Utopia!

All of the people living solitary existence's,
Whether by choice or circumstance,
Are missing the experiences that make life worth living;
My heart goes out to the lonely people that don't even know what they are missing.

December 25th, 1991

Poets over the years have attempted to describe love,
And all of the words that express this emotion are wholly inadequate.
To say that my love for you is boundless,
And that there has never been a person like you on the face of the earth,
seems to come close to what I feel;
But there are really no words that can express how much I Love you, my
wife.
The hope that you have given me,
The compassion you have provided to everyone you know, and me,
The warmth and tenderness that you exude,
The caring and concern you show for family an friends,
All these things make me Love you all the more.
My wife, you are the person I have dreamed of spending my life with.
You are by far the best lover I have ever known,
But this is really not as important to me as your other qualities.
It is your other qualities that make our joining that much the sweeter.

April 29th, 1992

The beginning of love has a way of bringing out the best of qualities in the prospect of man and woman.
When time has passed, and the love is still there, but some of the fire has been put on hold,
The doubts and concerns of the lovers seem to feed upon each other.

The best of all intentions may be overcome by the circumstances neither has control of,
But when the love is true, this must not be allowed to overshadow all else.
There is a way of rekindling loves passion, warmth, and compassion;
Share the fears and anxieties that sometimes become pent-up up within.
There is no better way of bringing back the togetherness, and fire of loves youth, than sharing your thoughts, feelings, and secrets.

May 9th, 1992

The beauty of each morning, with the suns rising,
Sometimes comes to soon for new lovers;
But with each new day comes the promise of a better tomorrow,
And the opportunity to improve on yesterday.

If the merest chance of having another to share your dreams and desires with comes your way,
All effort should be made to take advantage of that God sent opportunity.
Even if you are disappointed more times than not,
There is always the chance that it may work out.

May 16th, 1992

Forgiving the errors of bad judgment made in haste,
Takes a power of compassion and understanding that few possess,
And the fact that you are the one to blame, does not help.

There may be many valid reasons why there cannot be a good solution,
One that will answer the questions and fulfill the needs set forth.
The only real solution to the problems in life come from the heart, rather than the intellect.

Everything in life comes full circle to Love, Family, and Friends.
There is no substitute for having someone care for you more than they do themselves,
And to be able to reciprocate, makes the feelings shared practically perfect.

June 30th, 1992

Being of one mind, heart, and soul takes a special type of love.
The only way to accomplish this feat is to search diligently the world over for that match.
And if you should ever find that partner,
Never let them go.

The world is a hard place to face alone,
The only comfort that can be found is with the particular people that share your feelings,
And these are rare and far between.

Having the confidence to overcome the joys and heart breaks of getting to know another person,
Lasting out the bumps in the road to joining with another,
To make life both meaningful and satisfying,
Takes a mature frame of mind on both of your parts.

Loving someone as much as I love my wife, takes no effort at all,
Because she has the perfect frame of mind for me, and I for her.
When we met, I knew we would become as one,
To share all of our dreams and aspirations,
To help each other as no other couple has done before.
I believe this is the attitude that all marriages begin with,
But ours will be made to last our lifetimes and beyond, God willing.

June 30th, 1992
(Part B)

The beauty of having someone has no other comparison with anything that may be conceived by man.
When you are together, or apart, it is always for each other that you impart your thoughts,
And toward this continuing saga of love, hope and caring,
You will be forever together.

Happening to impart some words of wisdom,
Which have even a mild effect upon the development of another,
Gives one a sense of accomplishment and pride.

If there is no other reason to help another,
When the only recourse to helping, is ignoring the suffering,
Then help must be forthcoming, and from all.

July 3rd, 1992

Consoling the misguided people of this world with platitudes,
When what they really need is companionship and compassion.
Having the gall to judge others and sentence them without a thought to what harm this does,
Takes the type of maturity most often found in a 7 year old.

Perhaps there will be a time on this earth of ours,
When we will truly understand what it means to be brothers and sisters of the same family,
Humanity.
Then we might inspect our home, planet earth, and set to work cleaning up the mess we have of it.
Maybe this time will come, if we all start now.

July 5th, 1992
"Friends and Family"

Friends and Family are the people of this world with whom you share your love.
Coming to the realization that all the people of the world are just friends we haven't met as yet,
Is the universal truth that all must come to comprehend.
There are truly no bad people, only the misguided, and those whom do not know any other way.

Being one with all the living things of this earth, is how life was intended to develop,
But, somewhere along the way, hate, deceit, and mistrust entered into the equation,
And we all become victims of our greed, in one form or another.
The eternal hope that springs from the love of Friends and Family, gives rise to a multitude of possibilities.

We might have everlasting peace and fellowship upon the surface of this planet, our home.
There is the chance that all the cohabitants will come to love their neighbors as themselves.
There might be the opportunity to reshape the present and future along the lines intended.
The beginning of eternity just possibly could overwhelm the peoples of the earth.

(Undated)

Being in a state of anticipation, with the whole of the future ahead.
Having the awareness to realize that you have found the one person in the world meant for you,
And that person coming to the same realization;
This is what life is meant to be about, and all of those lost souls that do not come to this conclusion are to be pitied.

All of the possessions in the world may be showered upon you.
There may be nothing you lack for, except the peace of mind to enjoy them,
Because the coffers are full, does not mean that your heart is content.

The anxiety that people feel in today's society, springs from a lack of meaning in their personal lives.
The fault is not progress, but the concept that all is well if you have gotten your fortune,
No matter who was hurt by your success.
The ethics and morality of the "Golden Rule" has all but vanished from the life styles of men and women the world over.
There are always exceptions to any generalization, but there should be only peace on earth, and a willingness on the part of all to help the less fortunate.
When all is said and done, even if there is no accounting to your Maker at life's end,
What you have done to or for all the others sharing this mortal veil, will either praise or condemn you for all time to come;
Or you will not be remembered at all, and it would be as if you never existed.

July 14th, 1992

Having the will to do something about the loneliness felt by the majority, is the beginning,
Finding a way through the walls built by those that could fulfill your goal,
Takes the type of quiet determination that very few possess, and even fewer employ for a life time;
Help is needed from those individuals which are the most unwilling to come forward.

Finding the key to unlock the hearts, and open the minds of those you care most deeply about,
May be the most difficult task that you can ever undertake,
And the set-backs will sometimes seem to force you to give up, for a time.
Persistence in attaining your goal of smashing through the facade of protectionism held out to the world by about all people,
Will be rewarded, if the goal is even partially accomplished.

July 16th, 1992

Being in the majority of the tenets of this world,
Does have its' advantages with respect to getting along with your fellows,
And everyone needs to be as friendly with one and the other as possible,
But there comes a time when you shouldn't blindly imitate the thinking of the majority.

These are times when an injustice might be perpetrated,
Or if there is the chance that anyone might be hurt by such actions,
But remember above all that you must live with yourself for a long time,
And no one can make moral judgments for you that will work, except yourself.

"The Search"
July 17th, 1992

The beginning of awareness toward another,
Brings with it a responsibility to not injure either yourself or the other,
And if by chance, the other becomes enamored of you,
Then the start of wholeness is possible, with Love.

The problems encountered by most couples comes from outside influences,
Not of the times a couple spends together and alone.
And there is ample jealousy on the part of so called friends,
To bring asunder almost any budding relationship.

The bent of mind it takes to work at keeping together,
Must be shared by both, in order to have even a slight chance at maintaining a relationship.
And if you should drift apart from each other,
Simply count your blessings, and try again.

The most lonely of people never attempt to get back on the horse after the first broken heart they experience.
These are the ones that have not matured enough to realize that they are not a whole person without another to share all of life with.
And there are many such lost souls occupying this planet.
The chance of encountering them in your search is great, but be persistent, the end of the search is justifies all the heart break along the way!

July 20th, 1992

When the prospects of going through this world with blinders on to the rest of the inhabitants becomes to much.
If all you ever become involved with is your own problems and accomplishments,
Then you have missed the object of life and happiness.
For no one can be a whole person alone,
And if you think you can, you are not going to experience the joys of sharing your triumphs, and being consoled when misfortune strikes.
Because having another to share this life, feel for and with you, care for you and be cared for by you,
Can only be how to experience the full benefit of Love and friendship and family.

Undated (pre 1991)

There comes a time in the life of a bachelor when the pleasures of having time alone, pails.
And the need for companionship builds beyond the point of simple wants.
To alleviate this desire, it is necessary to become more of a caring person,
And to find that special person to fill your needs, and to in turn fill his/her needs as well.

You must be willing and eager to put the other person before yourself,
Or you are not going to have that happen for you.
Because if you do not care enough about his/her, he/she will eventually not care for you.
This is incontrovertible true, and it can happen to all, given time.

There are no guarantees with any budding relationship,
And you must work diligently at keeping truth and trust between you.
The alternative is not pleasant for either party,
And the courts are over loaded enough as it is.

Just because you have given a lady your name,
And signed all the papers necessary to be man and wife,
Does not mean that the privileges of matrimony will be continuous.
There well may be times when neither of you will be in the mood or unable to share these expressions of your Love on the physical plane.

When there may seem to be a lack of understanding,
And the once perfect couple that you started out being, appears to have dissolved,
Look at yourself first for the cause of this unhappy circumstance.
Then simply talk it out with the one you Love!

July 21st, 1992

Coming upon our first full month of wedded bliss,
We are truly thankful for all that we have together.
It is hard not to be able to share this feeling we have with everyone we meet.
But it is difficult to share this feeling with those that have never known the joy of the perfect match.

July 22nd, 1992

Coming to an understanding about how you feel for another,
And having the feelings shared as closely as possible,
Is the beginning; do not let frustration or mistrust enter into the equation.
Or what you have found may not survive for long.

July 23rd, 1992

Happening upon just the right person for you is almost a miracle,
But if you are one of the lucky ones, and you do nothing about it,
Then you have squandered an opportunity to be happy, and make other people happy as well.
Not just the one you found, but all the people that both of you encounter for the rest of your lives.

July 28th, 1992

Having the knowledge and wisdom of the ages at your disposal,
Does not preclude one from making the most fundamental of errors on the most trivial problems.
Common sense will help anyone, and most do not have the first clue to the concept.
But attempt to overcome this flaw with persistence, and you will be thankful when you do.

Undated (post 1991)

Nothing in this world comes easily, except Love,
You are born with the Love of your parents to sustain you,
And the continued acceptance of all your flaws by family,
Will go on past their time on this earth.

To take a family's caring for granted, and abuse it,
Is the most immature and selfish thing a person can ever do.
The type of person that does not understand when he hurts others that he is hurting himself more,
Does not belong in civilized society.

July 28th, 1992
(Part B)

The days of summer are numbered, and we should take full advantage of
the ones that are left.
The wonders of enjoying the warmth of the sun, the plush vegetation,
and the cool waters of lakes and rivers,
Will not continue through the Fall of the year and into Winter.
Take advantage of any opportunity that you feel is promising, and wait
not for tomorrow.

“Heaven on Earth”
July 28th, 1992

Being a Christian at any time in history has always been difficult.
The obstacles strewn in your path are many and treacherous.
From the self righteous hypocrites, to the ministers of so called Christian religions that are biased in their non-acceptance of other types of faith;
You will find that the Almighty God does not look kindly upon those who would be exclusive of all who believe and live by the teachings of Christ.

There was and is no better path to follow, than the trail laid down by the Son of God, so long ago.
The Hippies of the sixties and seventies were the closest to living the true Christian life in recent history,
But they were not accepted by society; in fact, they were abused and persecuted by so called Christians for their Loving and sharing way of life.
Even now, most people will not admit the fact that Christ was guiding that movement.

If you can truly call yourself a believer and follower of Christ,
Then more power to you, and spread that attitude to all you encounter down life’s path.
For the need for true Christianity has never been greater,
And the more people that practice it, the sooner we will have a **“Heaven on Earth”**.

"Thoughts"
July 31st, 1992

Thoughts of people with whom we have shared some time,
Come to mind with longings of a way to extend the good feelings shared.
With the hopes of spreading the camaraderie to more than just a few.
And bring companionship to all, whether they realize it is needed or not.

Only the time spent in preparation for sharing yourself with others,
Seems to be time that is better spent with friends, instead of by one's self.
If the time spent in solitude does any good at all,
It will make you appreciate that friends are a rare breed of people, and you should work at retaining all you possibly can.

When there is no further reason to continue with the life of a hermit,
You will find it difficult to match all your quirks with another.
But not so difficult as to be anywhere near impossible,
And every effort should be made to overcome any and all obstacles encountered.

For some, the search is long, and the path is winding and full of pitfalls,
For others, it seems they only have to look around the corner.
But to all, there is hope, and to give up completely is a crime.
So, be of a frame of mind that does not preclude an openness of heart and soul for your fellows, and you will find that sharing with another is by far more gratifying than being alone.

August 1st, 1992

Thinking of not being, and only wishing that the time will never come,
Accepting the fact that, as yet, there is no other alternative,
Then, living life to its' fullest while there is still time left,
Is becoming a rational adult, mature enough to enjoy the simple pleasures in life.

Having the wisdom to accept the ways of living in your time.
Being accepted by all that come to be acquainted with you, whether or not with liking;
And not being so insecure as to be threatened by others,
Will bring you good fortune and the chance of real happiness.

"Perception"
August 4th, 1992

Having the perception to see the faults of others;
Having the wisdom to keep your vision to yourself, when appropriate;
And giving your insights to others, if asked,
Is coming to the realization that there is no better way in which to help your fellow man.

All the prophets out of the history of man have attempted to help humanity,
With their special insights, garnered from their experiences and knowledge.
Without the acceptance of some higher authority,
All the knowledge and wisdom of the ages does little good.

When the wisest of the wise comes to understand the need for a belief in God;
And that understanding must be shared by all, in order to progress beyond the pettiness proliferated in this world;
Then the knowledge should be shared with all,
And perhaps then there will be the type of world that all would be proud to live in.

August 9th, 1992

Having accepted the role in life that seems to be pre-chosen for you,
Giving no further thought as to whether or not it is the correct choice,
Gives a feeling of peace and contentment that is seen and appreciated by all.
Do not get so complacent that your mind is closed to any other way of life.

The variety of differing occupations, avocations, and past times that is available in this time,
Are so numerous as to be uncountable,
And if you have not yet found your niche, be patient, for many are the people that will help you in your quest.
There are people whose life is laid out from birth, and then there are those that seem to drift aimlessly until death; try to make your life have some meaning.

When the time comes that you have encountered someone with whom you may wish to share your dreams,
Be prepared as best you can, with the compassion and understanding that will certainly be necessary,
To overcome all the obstacles that will surely present themselves in your paths.
There may be a better way of life, but marriage will have to do until it is revealed.

All of the wisdom of the world will do no good to a dishonest man.
No matter how many people he takes advantage of, he is really only cheating himself.
In all probability he will be lonely, even when surrounded by people,
And he will never be able to trust or Love another human, because he really does not trust or Love himself.

August 19th, 1992

The times in life that have little to do with sharing with another person,
Should be limited to introspection, in order to prepare yourself for what is to come.
So that you will be better able to appreciate what will surely come, if you have patience.
That is, you must surely find the person that you should share all of your dreams,
aspirations, and disappointments with, for that is how it is meant to be.

Lonely and full of anxiety are the times of people that do not make an effort to find a mate.
Wasted are the lives of those that remain unmatched,
Because there is no better way of life than marriage, family, and friends to share your time with.
All who think otherwise, are only fooling themselves.

Being of an attitude which precludes involvement,
And pretending to yourself that this is a happy existence,
Brings with time only loneliness and bitterness at oneself.
For you have missed the chance to continue your existence through the lives of others.

When the time comes that you should be ready to breathe your last breath,
And you have left no mark upon the hearts of others, except in passing;
Then your time on earth has not been well spent.
All the people that could have been loved by you, and that you could have affected, will have been lost to you forever.

"All My Love"
April 26th, 1992

Of all the wonders of the world, quite magnificent though they may be,
There is no greater feeling of amazement than the feeling that we have when we think of our one true Love,
And the Love that she has for us.

We may ponder what we have done to deserve the Love of such a lady;
It cannot be the way we are meticulous about some picayune problems or arrangement of household items;
It must be that she sees in us the Love that we have for her,
Our most wonderful Lady of our hearts.

August 19th, 1992

It was the afternoon conditions of cloudy skies, but no threat of rain.
That prompted me to think of pleasurable memories of years past,
When the age of my bones was not so great, and there was no worry about the rat-race that adults always seem to migrate toward.
Life seems to me better now, even though I am a part of the scuffle,
Because I have found my one true Love, and you should also count yourself lucky if you have found yours.

The people that still wonder when it will happen to them, have but to seek;
Because there is someone out there for everyone.
The only lonely people are those that choose to be that way, whether conscientiously or not.
There are to many excuses given by lonely hearts why they are still alone,
If they would really examine themselves, they would perceive that the only reason is their attitude toward new encounters.

When all the couples of the world have finally found each other,
Then there might just be the opportunity for the occupants of this planet to have "Peace on Earth",
That is what all of us Christians pray for, and each year at Yuletide time, we all profess to be working for it.
Much of the feelings and wishes that Christians have at Christmas time are really from the heart.
It seems that mostly all forget those feelings when the time of Christmas has past.

August 19th, 1992
(continued)

To attain the plateau of brotherhood on Earth, there must be sacrifices,
None of which should include those similar to what has been done before.
All should truly live the life of Christ to the best of their ability.
When this is done, there will no longer be any need for locks, security systems, or police.
There might be counselors to take the place of the people now occupying the judicial posts and law officers now prevalent.

The most important part of any dream of Utopia is having everyone share what true lovers have discovered;
If you do not know what that is, there are no words that might enlighten you,
You must seek that partner through the trial and error that all must go through to the longed for match.
When you have arrived at the destination intended, no one will have to tell you so.
There is no other feeling, thought, possession, or any other physical thing that compares!

August 30th, 1992

The sun has risen over the northern hemisphere, and all seems to be right with the world.
The appearance of tranquility which pertains to all Sunday mornings, when there is not to much commotion about the house or neighborhood,
Will persist through, hopefully, at least, the morning hours, and with luck the remainder of the day.
There is really only hope for a few of the church going population to become closely associated with the true path of Christ, and honestly decide to follow it.
There is always the chance with each Sunday morning, that more will endeavor to become as He.

When we decide to all go forth and do unto others as we would have them do unto us,
And this sentiment is shared world wide, then and only then, will there truly be peace on Earth.
Do not think that this begins with the other person, it must begin with you, for there to be any chance of it happening at all.
Give of yourself even if it hurts, to those that you perceive are in need of comfort,
And the rewards may not be instantaneous, but they will be forthcoming.

Of all the possibilities that prevail of the chance encounters that we all experience,
There just might be the chance that you will find a group, person, or couple, that live the life of happiness and Love that was intended for us all.
Be an outgoing, or at least not completely closed, individual, and share yourself with some others,
And hope and trust as much as you can in others,
Because no one can truly make it alone in the world at this time, or at any time.

Undated
(Pre 1991)

Going out into the world to make your own way,
Can be frightening, exciting, and something that should be shared.
All that can happen, and probably will, is that you learn what it is that you had,
And that your parents were not so stupid or uncaring, after all.

January 5th, 1993

Having the opportunity to present yourself in the best possible light,
Would you do so, knowing that you will have to live up to that office indefinitely?
Or would you rather be what you truly are, and be at ease with yourself and others?
Answer these questions, and when the time comes to choose, do so wisely.

January 6th, 1993

Sharing life's road with another,
And making a place for yourselves in the process;
May either be beautiful and simple, or ugly and difficult.
Making the right choice of a riding companion, is the key to determine one or the other path.

The lucky few that find the roadway to be smooth and without hazards,
Are those that realize and appreciate all that has and will be done for them by others.
There could be no unobstructed highways if there had not been those willing to set down the solid foundations.
When only a small percentage of the population does the work, only a very few will be appreciative of what it entails.

Dedicated to My Wife
January 7th, 1993

Of all the ladies of my acquaintance, both familiar and distant,
I find that there are only a few that hold my attention for very long.
Of that few, I have found only one, my wife, that could ever hold a candle to my ideal.
That candle's flame steadily becomes brighter and warmer as our time together lengthens.

The only wish that I hold close to my heart,
Is that my wife, my Love, my sweetheart, will stay with me forever.
There are no other reasons or explanations for the way I feel, towards her,
Other than Love, trust, and faith.

When our time on this earth is done,
And there are no longer any of our friends or family that can prolong our stay,
We will be satisfied and fulfilled with our time spent together.
So few ever share what we have been so privileged to find in each other!

My wish for the leaving of a legacy,
Is the hope for all that the friends we have made in our life together,
Will feel they have been helped by us, in some small way;
For that is what we both enjoy so much in the doing.

January 8th, 1993

Often we wonder why life has to be so seemingly difficult,
And most of us have thought this at one time or another.
So, by now, there should be an answer to this question that all could benefit by.
In fact there is no one answer, but so long as we ask the question, there is hope to make things less hard on ourselves and those around us.

January 9th, 1993

Traveling to the far corners of the globe in hopes of meeting someone of note,
Places hardships upon the body and soul of many.
There seems to be an over abundance of needless journeys,
But some are worthwhile, for people actually do find each other, despite all obstacles.

If there were sufficient reason for the necessity of travel,
Then all that has been wasted, is the time spend in indecision.
Of pondering this attitude, then that, and basically, shuffle footing around the inevitable.
All that needs be done, should be done to facilitate the quick rendering of a conclusion to the problems of the past.

"Couples"
January 11th, 1993

All things have relevance, when dealing with emotions,
And, hopefully, there are no hindrances to the truly manifold feelings between man and woman.
If a couple can withstand the all encompassing melee about them (sometimes called the "Real World"),
Then there is hope for all.

When outside influences are allowed to inject doubt and mistrust in the minds of either,
Is when the beginning of the end comes into play.
For there can be no "Happy Ever After", when there is not faith between a couple.
Beware the ill words, only meant to harm, coming from the jealous.

"The Journey"
January 14th, 1993

When the journey down life's highway becomes filled with pot holes,
And no matter where you attempt to detour, there seems no end to the rough ride,
Look around you, and appreciate what and whom you see.
Then thank your lucky stars that you have the friends and family around you that will stand up with and for you!

There will probably be no reason to begin even the shortest of journeys,
If the attitude one takes is negative in the first place.
Negativity only breeds more of the same, as it progressively goes along, with time.
When there are no other alternatives than to begin the journey, go into it with an open mind, and a Good Heart!

The results of visits to the past are sometimes unpleasant,
And there may be times when all that you hope to accomplish, does not work out.
There seems to be no reasonable alternative to bringing about better transactions than the ones foregoing the conclusions already persistent in your mind.
Help to overcome the errors made in youth, needs be brought up from within.

January 16th, 1993

When people become so self involved that nothing else seems to matter,
Then there is no reason to prolong whatever it is that keeps them so.
There should be a great coming of maturity, which will open their eyes
to the true meaning of Love!
That may be the only solution for us all!

January 22nd, 1993

When the world becomes as it should be,
And there no longer is strife among the peoples of all the nations,
There will be a great awakening to all.
The earth will be in unity, as it began.

The resulting world community will then be a true miracle to behold.
The Love that will prevail, should stomp out all hate and greed;
This will only occur when everyone shoulders the responsibilities upon themselves,
And learns to be considerate to all others.

“Emotions”
January 22nd, 1993

All emotions being of a somewhat equivalent nature,
There only remains the process of putting the best ones forward within.
Then sharing those with your fellow men and women.
So, that in the end, you would have lived your life with meaning.

January 24th, 1993

The world around us might seem to be falling to ruin,
But there will always be those bright spots that are populated by people who change your mind about that.
It does seem that those oases become further and further apart.
Although you should always be hopeful that they will multiply.

Being in a position to offer solace to the weary and down trodden,
You must take up the cause of helping all that you possibly can.
In order that those helped will, someday, return the favor to one's own.
If everyone took up this approach to their fellow man, it would eliminate a lot of grief on this planet!

Bringing together the friends and family that have accumulated to you,
Offers an opportunity to expand others' circle of friends,
And gives you the boon of knowing you have done something which may only be judged as good.
Have the courage to always do these types of things, and be of clear conscience about all others.

January 25th, 1993

The right to live in the environment of your choosing,
And not hold any other accountable for the choice,
Is, at best, ludicrous, unless you choose to be a complete hermit.
There seems, to the reasonable person, that in order to live in any environment, you must adapt to the surroundings in which you find yourself.
Those whom do not adapt, soon wither,
Or worse, take pleasure and meaning out of inventing petty vendettas against their fellow inhabitants.

"To an Exceptional Lady, Gwyndolyn Spencer" January 28th, 1993

There are few women in this world that deserve the title, Lady;
But, of those few, I have found that my wife, my mother, and Gwyndolyn, are of their highest ranks.
When the pressure of everyday living gets to me at work,
There is always the warm, friendly, and compassionate aspect of Gwendolyn's company for all whom but ask for it.

I consider Mr. Spencer to be one of the very few lucky men,
That are fortunate enough to find such exceptional Beauty in a member of the opposite sex.
And, being one of those few, I fully appreciate what this means.
My hope for you both, is that your future is as trouble free as such a fine couple only has the right to expect.

January 30th, 1993

Living in a world of greed, that seems to be nothing but trouble for those in need,
And having nothing to show for years of labor at a particular task,
May have either detrimental or inspirational affect upon the human spirit within us all.
Have faith in your fellow man, and cease to long for things that really have no meaning, outside the bounds of the soul;
Because therein lies the seed to force a new beginning upon the race toward Utopia.

"All Things, Big and Small"

There comes a time when there is so much to consider, that there seems no time to cover it all.
When that period comes to you, try not to think to heavily upon the consequences of your actions as they might affect you,
But upon what your actions mean to the ones around you.

If after all this is taken into account, and you still see no alternative to the present situation,
Then, drop back fifteen yards, and punt;
Because if you follow the above guidelines, and fail to come to a satisfactory resolution,
You were not paying very good attention.

January 31st, 1993

Going through the motions of life, pretending to yourself that this is the way it should be,
Is one of the biggest lies that man tells himself, and there is no reason for the deception.
Especially when there is an alternative to the struggle of mundane existence, we call living in the real world.
There is Love and Brotherhood among almost all in the perfect world,
And you only have to look in order to find it.

January 31st, 1993
(Part B)

Having the wherewithal to endure all comers, and still come up smiling,
Takes a perspective on life that is at one and the same time optimistic and realistic.
Friends that are not in any way a burden, but a blessing, also helps.
Knowing whom your true friends are, makes all the difference in the world.

"Utopia"

The beginning of eternity starts now,
And there is no better time to prepare than the present.
Ask only of yourself and others, what you feel in your soul to be just and fair,
And you have taken the first major step.

All over the world, people have searched for a reason to go on with the seemingly endless struggle of finding peace,
But, up until the current era, there hasn't been the prospect of a world community to draw upon.
Now, there is that world community and there should be no reason for not having peace throughout the earth.
All those that favor this scenario, should put all their efforts into the realization of this magnificent dream.

Love is the key to the everlasting heaven on earth,
And all those not in favor, should simply keep quiet.
With Love of self and your fellow man,
An ever continuing Utopia could not help but rein.

February 2nd, 1993

Being in the right perspective of mind with the perfect mate,
Can be the most beautiful thing in the world.
Having the wisdom and luck to perceive these two,
Is truly a gift from above.

The fortunate few which realize happiness in each other,
Should thank whatever Lord they worship for all the joys of togetherness.
And of all the endless pleasures of sharing themselves with each other.
Be thankful, for the majority are not so lucky.

"Becoming One"
February 2nd, 1993

Becoming one, begins with the infatuation of first encounter,
And grows or withers according to the Lord's will.
Having the opportunity to attempt a union,
Comes to all of God's creatures at some time in their lives.

Actually finding someone of the perfect attitude and personality for you,
Takes a lot of luck and work, to accommodate each other.
There is no substitute for having the perfect someone.
When no one else seems quite right, you know in your heart and mind
they are for you what Romeo was for Juliet.

“Possessions”
February 5th, 1993

Of all things, large and small, the most familiar are often the best pleasing.
There are often times those of us that would want more than we could afford,
But there may be other means to put those things within our grasp.
Although, like as not, we may not truly appreciate and care for those possessions after they have been acquired.

February 7th, 1993

Nothing of this world should so over rule your thoughts as to cause tension or anxiety,
And if you should ever become so self involved that no amount of reason or logic holds sway,
Do not be surprised at the reactions caused by your attitude.
Especially if there is no one with whom to share your thoughts and feelings.

Luckily, most of us have someone to act as a sounding board,
For those which do not, have sympathy and understanding.
They are lost in a world of their own self involvement,
And cannot be held completely responsible for their own actions or words.

"Alone"
February 10th, 1993

Being with the one you Love and have decided to spend the rest of your life with,
Is the most beautiful prospect ahead of all of us.
And there is absolutely no substitute for your perfect match to travel life's highways with.
All that is needed on both your parts, is the acceptance of each and the others' personalities.

If you should wonder, when there is a time of hardship,
Whether or not you made the right choice,
Look into your innermost soul and try to recapture what was there when you joined with that other.
If you still have doubts, then the union may not have been right in the first place.

"Life's Avocation"
February 13th, 1993

Finding one's avocation, and not acting upon the realization of its' aspect,
May be the one unforgivable, to themselves, sin that people find in their consciences.
If you should be both fortunate and gifted, act upon your instincts.
Be stubborn enough to follow through with whatever it takes to be true to yourself.

"Valentine's Day"
February 14th, 1993

On Valentines Day of any year, a man's thoughts should always turn to his most cherished partner.

If he does not have one, more is the pity, for man is incomplete without a woman.

There is no more esteemed state of life, than matrimony with the right lady.

Having the extreme good fortune to find the Love of your life, is one of God's greatest miracles, not to be scoffed at or treated lightly.

The wonder of sharing your life with a perfect soul mate, partner, lover, and friend, is what is called marriage.

There is no Holier institution than marriage outside of the church;

And not that many of today's churches are practicing what the good Lord intended for them anyway.

Living in the real world, and not having the spouse that will make all the mundane chores seem joyous,

Is like never having sweets or spices in your diet, you never come to understand what pleasures there are in life.

So, find that someone who will always be there for you, and share whatever it is that life is putting you through.

There is no other way of life that is quite so blessed, and quite so meaningful, as marriage.

"Position"
February 15th, 1993

Being in a position of power, be it of wealth or leadership, has peculiar effects on those so honored.
And if not careful the heights attained may ruin even the best of original intentions.
Wariness of to much pride will assist in keeping things in prospective;
And helpfulness to, and involvement in the welfare of others can never hurt.

February 15th, 1993
(Part B)

Having nothing to lose but time and effort, any endeavor is better than complacency and blind acceptance of the way things are.
If nothing strikes you as worth doing, then do nothing;
But be prepared to accept the consequences of inaction, and indifference to your plight by others.
There is no excuse for planning your life in a vacuum, and then complaining about the lack of air.
The old homilies of the “Golden Rule”, and having the wisdom to attempt change of injustices,
Are just as valid today as they were at their inception centuries before.
Have the faith in your fellow man to give everyone the benefit of a doubt.
Do not underestimate the power of positive reinforcement of the good in others.
You may be disappointed many more times than not,
But even if only one out of a million turns around,
Then all of it will have been worth the while.
Do not kill the faith in the basic goodness of humanity by turning away from those in need of you.

February 16th, 1993

Going to extremes in anything may be the worse thing which you can do for yourself and others.
There is nothing worse than a person whom will not take pause and enjoy what he is doing,
Rather than setting about every aspect of his life in a dead serious plane.
Take the lessons that life has to offer with an attitude which will allow you to smell the Roses along the way.
Do not think that you are the only one that counts or has problems, when things don't go exactly your way,
Because everyone has their cross to bare.
Do not accept the status quo in your life, make waves.

"Living the Life"
February 17th, 1993

Of coming to an understanding of yourself, which does not involve others,
There can be only one concept that stands out, you cannot live a life worth while without others.
Do not be discouraged if at first there is no reason or rhyme to your attempts at joyous living;
Because there is not enough time allotted to each individual to meet all the people that one would wish to.

Have faith in yourself and others, in order that you may come to appreciate what is on this planet.
Do not be negative in your outlook on the world as it is,
Because it its only what we, as a race, have made of it.
All the things you do not like, make every effort to better understand, and hopefully, change.

When the planet Earth has finished its' time in the Universe,
There may be other places for the human race to inhabit.
Do not let it concern you over much, there is plenty of time left to reinvigorate this old world.
Have the good sense to understand the things that need changing, and do that which most facilitates a meaningful result.

Having the right attitude toward life and how it should be lived,
Is the hardest thing that anyone can come to know about themselves.
Not becoming depressed when your plans go astray,
Is the only way to truly understand yourself, with an aspect toward others that is helpful, when possible.

February 17th, 1993
(Part B)

On the Seventh Day of the rest of your life,
There should be a complete comprehension of what it is that makes you happy, sad, and indifferent.
If the concept does not appeal to you, then ignore it,
For the only people this is for, is myself and my wife.

February 18th, 1993

Accounting for the differing possibilities involved in developing a conscience,
Most people discover that, no matter what obstacles stand in the way, it is easier than not having one.
Because no person can stand alone for very long without faltering,
There is a basic need for a justifiable way of living with your fellow man.

February 19th, 1993

Being in a position where whatever you do seems not quite correct,
And not knowing whether or not anything that occurs from the result of your actions will harm, rather than help,
Has a tendency to put one on the edge of indecision about the most mundane of matters.
The only way I have found to overcome this dilemma of perspective, is to take time out.

February 19th, 1993
(Part B)

People have a talent for overstating the obvious.
Those that say not enough, are at least listened to when they do speak;
But the happy median is the most difficult to attain.
Very few ever achieve this in their own eyes, and fewer still, in the eyes of others.

February 19th, 1993
(Part C)

Have the patience to understand what has gone before,
And have the wisdom to comprehend that it should not be repeated, if not so desired.
Having the pure knowledge of what should be, but is not,
Is not enough; you must actively seek to enjoy changing the status-quo for the better.

February 20th, 1993

Being of one mind with another is the most difficult aspect of living together in a relationship.
The ideal must be worked on and reworked, until both are in accord.
There is no substitute, or nearly "just good enough" facsimile,
For true Love, there must be total compliance between the two of you.

February 21st, 1993

Becoming one with whatever person you choose to live your life with,
Can be the single most important aspect of saving what is left of your soul.
Because there is no better life than the one shared with another,
Find the compassion and understanding within yourself to accomplish this feat.

Be of calm demeanor toward others with not so patient an attitude.
Have compassion for all the hungry souls you encounter,
That have no concept of what true Christian Love is.
We all go through these phases of doubt, and most of us take our frustration out on the innocent.

The faint of heart will never quite come to grips with their conscience,
And all that they lack in understanding is made up for, within themselves, as vindictiveness and pettiness.
Do not fall into the trap that is so easily lain,
And treat the other people in your life as badly as you sometimes treat yourself.

February 22nd, 1993

Of all the experiences with people of differing walks of life,
I have found that the people of the country are the best.
They have a home spun honor and pride of workmanship unsurpassed,
And these are truly the backbone of America.

There is no faltering when they give their word.
There are no other substitutes for having them come to you with their pride intact,
To ask or question your motives in ail you do.
If ever you cross one of these chosen people, beware, for they seldom forget an injustice.

They are not unforgiving, but they will be wholly cautious in future dealings,
And the trust they exude will not be quite as readily forthcoming.
Have your honor ready on the line, and you will not do badly.
Never give false witness to a friend or acquaintance, because that is one thing that is not easily forgiven!

February 23rd, 1993

Having the tenacity to understand just what is meant by people who speak the truth,
And not underestimating those with less education than themselves,
Is the essence of becoming a better humanist than the self proclaimed leaders of "The Faith" seen on every TV station and most pulpits, every Sunday.
So, do not just blindly follow those with seemingly pat answers, find your own.

To Paul, wherever he is, on his birthday. February 23rd, 1993

Paul is the type of individual which succumbs to all kinds of escapism.
He does, or did, just not like the fact that he was simply not quite as bright as some of his siblings,
So, he rebelled against facing the truth of his shortcoming, in his mind, by taking drugs and alcohol every day.
My hope for this wayward brother is that he has learned to accept himself for what he is, and not for his picture of what he should be!

February 23rd, 1993
(Part C)

Substituting false courage for what should be there from the start,
Can only bring about misery to yourself and others close to you or not so close.
When the rat race gets you down, look inward or upward, but not to a bottle,
For the only solace found in a bottle, your self respect should be able to do without.

Having the courage not to let peer pressure bring about dismay,
And letting no one else discover your frailties of self image,
Can only make you a lonely and independent person.
It takes another person to share those peculiarities of self, that make you fit company.

Being right, does not always mean parading your correct solution in the face of others;
But it does give on self confidence in the otherwise self doubt of the inner mind.
Be what you are, and have the courage to project that self to others.
Hiding behind a false facade does no one good!

February 25th, 1993

Having the fortitude to withstand all inconvenient rules of the game of life,
And still maintain a cheery outlook on the other aspects of living,
Behooves one to have a very understanding and forgiving nature.
But even a saint can only take so much.

Giving up all semblance of culture and pride of society,
And having nothing to replace It with, except anarchy,
Is no method that can be made to work for anyone, unless they are solitaire.
Have patience with those less fortunate than yourself, and do not wish to be left alone, you might get that wish.

February 26th, 1993

All of the hopes for a better tomorrow are would up in the longings of today,
And no amount of wishing will bring those hopes to pass, without work.
There may be simple answers to all your questions,
But do not depend on someone else for them, you must find your own.

Have persistence in looking for the right type of mate to share your dreams with,
And all else will simply fall into place in your life.
Not possessing an attitude of superiority over others is an important plank in being whole.
Maintaining a willingness to assist others in their goals will stand you in good company.

Be the type of person that can make lemonade when life hands you lemons.
Do not bemoan your fate while doing nothing about changing it.
Hard work is still the only cure for bettering your future;
And no easy answers are worth very much in the long run.

All things being equal under the light of reason,
And no one thing having precedence over another,
Will more than likely, always be true.
In the long haul, after your time is spent, only your Maker and whatever family and friends you leave behind will have remembrance of what you would have accomplished in life.

February 26th, 1993
(Part B)

The starting point of any relationship is awkward, at best;
But whatever comes of a first encounter, it is better to make the attempt, than not.
Have the persistence to include every effort possible in the attempts made in that direction,
And, whether the results please both of you or not, at least you have given it a chance.

Giving to another what you would wish for yourself,
And having the other appreciate the thought that went behind the gift,
Is a special thing, and should be cherished to your heart and not easily forgotten.
Having a gift really appreciated these days is no mean feat.

Take solace when and from whom you can,
Because there is no substitute with self pity for the understanding of another.
Do not be so independent of nature that you over look the gifts given to you by others;
Such as their time, concern, and attention to your needs.

February 27th, 1993

All of God's children, including you, have problems that need to be worked out within themselves.
Having no other resources than themselves, is not conducive to healthy problem solving.
The shared approach to working out dilemmas of conscience is always best;
Unless you cause problems for someone else, or do not receive the correct input from the other.

Being alone most of the time, can only bring unhappiness to you and those close to you,
For you have not given your loved ones much in return for their concern for you.
No amount of regret will make up for moments that could be spent together,
Embracing one ant the other with body and soul.

Having someone Love you, makes life all the sweeter,
And gives everyone reason enough to go on with the business of living to the fullest.
But sparse moments alone are not all bad,
For you do need time to gather your thoughts and feelings into cohesive ways of expressing them.

To My Wife
after eight months of marriage.
February 27th, 1993

An understanding wife is what every man dreams about having.
Most will never attain this with their spouse,
But I have been given the most understanding of ladies, my wife,
To share with and have share all the wonders of Love and life.

There may be many ladies around the world that would suit many men,
But the most wondrous of Ladies is now my wife, and unattainable to others.
Having no thought of ever separating from this eight wonder of my world,
I would only hope that every day of our lives we say those three words to each other, “I Love You”.

Simple are our pleasures in each other,
And complicated are our feelings toward each other.
With the foundation of two caring, compassionate, and loving people in this marriage,
We will weather any storm which comes along with each other to depend upon.

Of all the women of my knowledge, there are not very many to compare,
With my wife’s loving nature, or her attitude about all aspect of Love and family.
Everything in our lives is coming together with both of us working toward each others’ goals.
Almost, in perfect unison we teach our friends what marriage is supposed to be about.

I believe that there are some few other couples that might have almost attained what we possess in each other,
But I do not think that any other couple will ever be able to completely inspire each other in the way we do.
There are only those few closest friends that understand what is shared by us;
And appreciate what a beautiful relationship we have.

February 27th, 1993
(Part C)

To look unending for the perfect match is a full time occupation for some of us.
Most people seem to look in the wrong places or so it might seem.
The trick to any successful search is to forget about looking so much,
And just let the fates and intuition take over.

September 7th, 1992

Coming to the realization that there is no better place to be than the home we have all searched for;
With the people that mean the most to us surrounding us with their Love and friendship,
Is a coming of age in this world of casual acquaintances and encounters that do not last the day.
Having the wisdom to appreciate what most take for granted is a God given gift that should not be squandered.

Finding happiness with what you have, and not always wishing for something more.
Giving thanks even when things do not go as well as you would wish.
Sharing what little you have with others even less fortunate.
All this is what life in its' purest is supposed to be.

Having the good sense to understand that no one can survive in this hard world alone.
Having the good fortune not to have to attempt this feat of being apart from humanity,
Is a gift that can only be given by another, whether you are worthy of that gift or not.
The great secret of life might be accepting what is given freely, and rejecting that which comes with strings.

September 12th, 1992

Concern over loved ones and their frailties, might give rise to self doubt about your ability to help in any way,
Being as supportive as possible, and attempting to understand and forgive any misunderstandings of the past,
Brings back the feelings of togetherness which should be the only concern in their hour of need.
After all, family and loved ones are what truly matter in this world, and all effort should be made to reconcile these people in your world as they should be.

Having the frame of mind that it takes to hold a family together is a special bent of mind that should be cherished.
Every opportunity should be taken to practice this upon society, but especially with family and friends.
There really should be no ill feelings between you and all else around you.
Those types of feelings do nothing for anyone concerned, and should not be allowed to fester.

September 26th, 1992

Becoming as one with the partner of your journey through life, may be the ultimate goal of all relationships.
Not putting any pressure on either party is the easiest method to this end.
Letting yourselves share whatever is on your minds, and being open to the others' thoughts, dreams, and aspirations,
Helps along the road to commitment to each other, and will lead to a fruitful future.

Having the fortitude to withstand the temptations of outsiders, and the burdens sometimes put in the way,
Takes a special understanding and maturity to overcome, and build upon the foundation of what has passed, hitherto.
Of all the possibilities that might come to pass in a relationship, the only thing that should matter is whether both are happy.
If both are improved by the partnership, then all effort must be made to withstand all that comes against it.

“Thanksgiving”
November 26, 1992

Considering all the possibilities of what life would be like without the benefit of family and friends to assist in the struggle,
Would seem to give almost everyone reason to be thankful, at any time of the year, and especially now.
All of the supposed injustices perceived to be done to you by others, will only bring sorrow to you if allowed to fester within.
So, be thankful for whatever you have: health, friends, and family, because being unappreciative of these will make you sour, and not very good company.

Of the things I have to be thankful for, the foremost in my thoughts is my loving wife.
There are couples that share this feeling together, and of those I know only a few;
But that is no reason to think that you will not be able to find that special someone.
Just be thankful that you have the chance to look.

If hope seems to be vanishing, and the goal of the search has eluded you,
Look outside yourself, for there are only the most worthwhile answers to your questions with interaction with others.
People that consider themselves and their problems of the upper most importance at all times,
Only put a drag on themselves and the people they come into contact with.
So, be considerate of others, and don’t get to tangled in the web of troubles that we all must endure.

September 1st, 1992

Awaiting the outcome of the events set in motion by previous action;
Not wanting to become to enamored of personal ability, or inability;
Having the good sense to understand that there is no reason for anyone to feel inadequate with themselves;
And at the same time realizing that to find a level of comfort with oneself is the goal prior to the ultimate of a comfort zone with another.

Being with friends is a step;
Being with the one you love, and with friends, is the next step;
Having all: friends, family and the one you love surround you with their caring and concern,
Is what life at it's best is all about.

Finding the right person is so difficult for most people,
Because they will not let themselves be open to new encounters.
The first step is to trust yourself enough not to be afraid of what might be around the corner.
Give everyone at least one chance, but with most, it will take more than one.

August 28th, 1992

Misery, as the old saying goes, loves company.
Don't get so engrossed in your own frustrations that you overlook the possibility of there being a brighter tomorrow.
When every day coping with all the "small stuff" becomes to much,
Just observe the trees and God's green earth, and be thankful for what you have.

All over the world there are people that come to the point in their lives when nothing seems to matter anymore.
They feel useless and worthless, and sometimes contemplate not have to face it anymore.
Taking the coward's way out is definitely not the solution, it only creates more problems for the ones you care about.

The problems experienced by most of us lies with how we handle our frustrations.
Most of us don't handle them at all, we just let them build until there is no longer a good way of releasing them.
That is when the explosion of thought and emotion takes over, and the outcome is not pretty.
With any luck at all, we might wind up getting the help needed to cope, but someone in our lives must help us to seek out this possibility.

There is hope for any and everyone, but there must be an understanding on the part of those closest of what is needed.
There can be no pretending the problem is all on the others' part;
The problem is to penetrate the wall of defense mechanisms put in the path of unpleasantness by most of us,
So that we will be forced to face the real problems and find real solutions to those problems.

December 15th, 1992

The bliss of being with someone that will share your laughter, joy and love,
While still having the compassion and understanding to help you get through your times of sorrow,
Is someone so special that no matter how long the wait before you encounter,
You should not settle for anything less, because you do both parties an injustice.

Having waited my life, until of forty, for the one person who fit my image of a mate,
Was well worth all the bad times, loneliness, and despair which came before.
There is no substitute for a spouse that you truly love and who loves you in return.
Project you true self at all times, warts and all, and there is no doubt that you will find that someone.

My Wife
(Undated)

Loving someone as much as I love my wife, takes no effort at all.
She has the perfect frame of mind and heart for me, and I for her.
When we met, I knew we would become as one,
To share all of our dreams and aspirations,
To help each other as no other couple has done before.
I believe this is the attitude that all marriages begin with,
But ours will be made to last our lifetimes and beyond, God willing.
The beauty of having someone, such as my wife, has no other comparison with anything that may be conceived by man.
When we are together, or apart, it is always for each other that we impart our thoughts.
Toward this continuing saga of Love, Hope, and Caring, my wife and I will be forever building our relationship together.

March 1st, 1993

The realization of past misdeeds, that can no longer be made right,
Brings with it a guilt that may harm your happiness, and upset your conscience.
Have regret that these things happened, but go on with your life.
No amount of guilt or regret will ever undo what has already been done.

March 1st, 1993
(Part B)

Coming to some understanding of why you behave the way you do,
And going beyond assigning blame, to making valid efforts to adjust your behavior,
Is the healthiest attitude to take towards living with and for yourself and others.
The trap is to only blame the past, and not live in the present.

March 1st, 1993
(Part C)

All the children of the world, both young and old,
Have one thing in common, they do not wish to grow up quickly or at all.
Not to say that all young children are this way,
But the ones which have problems, will not accept responsibility for themselves.

The simple answers for these children are long since past.
Now, they will have to seriously adjust their methods of interaction with others.
They will need a stable environment, and good roll models.
The only lasting way they will be helped, is if they do it themselves.

March 2nd, 1993

Of all the people I have met, during a life time of seemingly aïmless wanderings,
But a few stand out in contrast and memory as being of note.
Those few will know whom they are, and not merely by my mentioning them,
But by their understanding of how I relate to them, both now and in the past.

Having a friend or two that would not but bring joy to your day,
And holding no grievances against those that do not really understand you,
Brings with it a contentment of soul and heart and mind, that is at once peaceful and anticipatory.
You must always be on guard against having over confidence, that would turn to hurtful pride.

Take into your heart those that both deserve your attention, and those that need your help.
Have no thoughts which bode ill for any but yourself;
Additionally, do not be overly critical of yourself, either,
For, without understanding of oneself, there can be no understanding of others.

Having come to some type of arrangement with yourself about your short comings,
And still loving yourself; others will then have a chance with you, too.
The good that can be done is no insignificant thing,
So, be kind to yourself and the others in your life will appreciate it.

March 3rd, 1993

Coming of age in this world of fast paced morals and loose scruples,
Must be the most difficult part of growing up that any young person has to face.
There are not many that mature unscathed by the drug and alcohol users which abound.
It is a miracle that more of our youth do not succumb to the pressures to try these harmful escapes.

Having the only method of avoiding these pitfalls, a good family,
Even the best of our youth experiment with what they justify as being harmless.
There are no completely harmless illegal or legal drugs that can be used.
Those that think they can get away with abusing their bodies and minds are fooling only themselves and destroying their families.

Being with the people you care most about,
And not being in control of your own mind and body,
Is the most selfish aspect of drug abuse that users don' seem to understand.
They are simply trading a harmful escape from seeming intolerable reality, with an even worse substitute.

The answer for these people of decaying mind and body,
Is for them to come to the realization that no temporary escape with drugs,
Will substitute for the natural high of Love which Family and true Friends provide.
The type of friends found in the abusive cultures will provide little substance on which to found any meaningful kind of Love.

March 4th, 1993

Those of us which feel for others' misfortunes,
And attempt to make things easier for them,
Have rough sailing over choppy waters with most.
There are those that make the waters as smooth as glass, though.

Having the right attitude toward others, and being in the correct frame of mind,
Will help you in all endeavors of mind, body and soul searching for the answers to your questions concerning life.
Being with someone of similar aspect that is not afraid to ponder these questions,
Will bring about a rapport which might lead to eternal happiness for you both.

Have hope and faith that your dreams will come to fruition.
Look not upon what has happened previously in your life that was not good,
But recall those memories which were joyous and meaningful,
And you will wonder about how to make your present similar to those times.

The Good Lord, in all of His mercy, has seen fit to bestow upon us as many opportunities as needed,
For we poor mortals to follow in His footsteps, that lead to true peace.
There are many methods to accomplish His goals;
Choose the path that most nearly resembles His, and you will not be very far from right.

March 5th, 1993

Coming to an understanding and Love of yourself,
Is the major part of preparing yourself for the Love of another.
No matter what you think to the contrary, there is no substitute for the Love, faith, and compassion a mate bring into your life.
To settle for less in a relationship, is to do an injustice to both.

A token of Love that may be shared by a couple,
Is best exemplified by the sharing of compassion and understanding with all you meet.
No amount of otherwise unruly action, will cause friction between you both.
Do not fall for the green-eyed monster's trap, but have faith and trust in each other.

Have the audacity to bring you Love of life into your associations with all the people you come into contact with.
There may or may not be the necessity of preliminary encounter, that depends on the others;
But, whatever you do, do not hide behind walls that shut out all,
For you will miss the golden opportunities ahead.

March 5th, 1993
(Part B)

When traversing any new path on the landscape of life,

You should keep in mind that others have probably gone before you, and others will probably follow.

The key to any new experience is to keep an open mind, while at the same time keeping your goal in sight.

Do not be of the type to litter the path with your left over rubbish, and you should do well in any new endeavor.

March 6th, 1993

Throughout the eons of Man's ascendancy to dominance of this planet, earth,
There has been only one species that challenged his preeminence, Man himself.
It is such a foolish struggle of Nation against Nation, and differing religions against each other.
There should be some understanding and tolerance of others' beliefs, instead of Man's over powering urge to bend others to his beliefs and will.

Having said that there should be a method for all Men and Women to live in harmony together,
There should be a concerted effort towards that end by All.
When there is the maturity of our species that allows this conjunction of minds and wills,
Then the accomplishments that we will be afforded, will astonish us all.

Being, without a doubt, the only reasoning species occupying this world,
There is no logical reason for us to quarrel amongst ourselves.
All that is that causes these quarrels is selfishness and greed.
There is no room for these things in the mature minds and hearts of good people!

What we may do as individuals is to live our lives with each other without strife.
There is no reason for us to struggle with each other over so unimportant things as material possessions,
And if we could all understand this logic, all would be well with the rest of the world.
There would be no more border disputes or attempts by some nations to dominate others or take away their freedom and lands.

March 7th, 1993

Upon a Sunday morn, there should be no strife between man and woman.
Since this is the day of rest and peace among most civilized people,
When there comes an interruption of tranquility, whether by outside influence or not,
There must be a leveling of emotions between each spouse.

Having all the Love for each other that you possibly can,
Still does not give warrant to excluding one from the other any secrets of feelings.
If you cannot share all that is clear to you both,
Then perhaps you should not have begun the relationship.

Of all the couples that we have known,
my wife and I only share ourselves with a few.
Those few are the ones we care most dearly about,
Because they care for each other and all that they associate with.

Being with a Lover, Friend, and Companion throughout your life,
Who will give to you, freely, all that you desire from another person,
Is a miracle of Love, and should not be abused, no matter the excuse.
Having a special someone, does not give license to anyone!

March 7th, 1993
(Part B)

Share with your fellow man and woman what you hold dear to yourself,
And if those things you cherish are of true worth,
You will all be rewarded for the interaction.
When only material things are of worth, you may be surprised at how shallow your friends are.

There can be no justification for not helping your brother or sister, when possible.
Those that selfishly guard all their time and possessions to themselves,
Are missing out on the glories of living.
If you find that the only reason you get up in the morning is to bring to yourself more gold, you are not truly living.

Give to those that would wish it, all that you possess,
And if you don't know what will become of those possessions, all the better.
Simply because you once owned something, and it was nice,
Does not mean that it will be yours forever, unless that possession is True Love.

The ecstasy and agony of True Love are felt by all, at some time e in their lives.
They may not admit to themselves or others that it did,
Because they have determined that it was a temporary weakness on their part,
And the hurt has made them deny it!

March 7th, 1993
(Part C)

Going to the trouble to express yourself in writing has it's advantages,
You do not have to exert much effort in speech, and writing allows more time to formulate your thoughts.
Do not give up speaking, but for feelings or thoughts that mean a lot to you,
The written word is sometimes better, and always more meaningful.
Oral communication is her in the present, but cannot be held onto for very long.
When the great men of history formulated their thoughts, it was always written first.
Since the beginning of recorded history, writing has been an honored profession,
And all those that choose this profession or calling, are people of great introspection and, also, have an understanding of human values and needs.
There have been abusers of this intellect: Hitler, and others.
For the most part, those whom understand human nature, in all it's frailties,
Do not abuse that knowledge, knowingly.
The psychiatrists of our time are men and women of intellect and learning,
But they often abuse that power with the feeling that they know what is best for everyone.
Far be it from me to pass judgment on all, indiscriminately,
But Doctors, Lawyers, and most Men of the Cloth, feel they have a special gift or knowledge which makes them everyone's leader.
Most of these self professed leaders of Men would not know truth if it bit them on their derrieres,
So, make all judgments only upon yourself,
And if you wish to share the knowledge you have gained,
Do so without commanding that others do likewise.
There are no answers that fit all people the same,
And the sooner everyone realizes this, the better off the world will be!

March 8th, 1993

Seeing all the injustices that are prevalent throughout the world,
And feeling helpless to participate in some manner to correct them,
Leaves one with a frustration and agony of spirit that will afford no solution.
The only real answer is to help when possible, and attempt to understand where not.

Life is sometimes unfair to the caring individual,
And there seems no corresponding logic that will explain why not.
When this happens, it is most often because of the greed or selfishness of others,
And there is no good reason for that on the part of any.

Being one of the caring individuals in the species,
And not having a care about how your time is spent with regard to others needs,
Will force you into the mode of over extending yourself, unduly.
The time spent helping others, is time very well expended.

Have empathy for your fellow's plight,
And hold no superior attitude over another,
For you could be in the same predicament someday.
And only the luck of the draw keeps things going for us all.

March 10th, 1993

Going about the day's business, with no thought of tomorrow's cares,
Does have advantages for some.
It leaves all planning for the future in an abyss of thoughtlessness,
And there is no security in that.

Planning over much for the future can lead to a dullness of living,
And will take most pleasure out of life;
But all spontaneity and no forethought is not good, either.
So, learn to practice both in moderation.

Have the common sense to distinguish between good planning and luck,
And if, by chance, you should have the good fortune of finding the correct path,
Don't be so selfish that you exclude all others from your good luck.
Let others in on the secret, but don't demand that they do likewise.

Being alone is never good for long periods,
When you have attained the necessary partner for life,
Then all effort should be made to satisfy both your needs for togetherness.
Do not exclude her from any aspect of you life, for then comes the agony of leaving things unsaid.

March 13th, 1993

Coming to understand what your life is about,
And not comprehending the lack of the same realization by others,
Gives a person pause, to consider all the aspects of living that are often taken for granted.
These are a few of the times that make us look inward for some ulterior motives.

Give thanks that you have the freedom to think and speak as you will,
And don't be self pitying about all you don't have.
There are places where, no matter what you have, you would not be so privileged.
There may be good reason for you to want more, but first be thankful for the small things you have.

Having all the riches that you ever thought were attainable to you,
And not wondering why you couldn't have more,
Will, perhaps, force you to give reasoning to your thoughts about others,
And all they lack in that area.

There is a lot even the poor in this country can do toward helping the starving children of the world,
And there is no other country in the world that has so much as we.
So, think about what you can do to make things better, at least for those you know.
That is your obligation to your fellow man and woman.

March 13th, 1993
(Part B)

If you should find a person the Love in this life,
Give to them all that you would like to have given to you.
You shall receive all that you have dreamed possible.
And, maybe a little more if the lover you have chosen is the right one for you.

The wonders of a True Love affair with a good person,
Is a miracle to behold throughout the ages.
No one should take that miracle for granted,
Because it only happens once or twice in a lifetime, if at all.

Don't be so cynical that you by pass all that is good in people,
And you will come to understand what real living and loving are about.
It is not what you can get, but what you can give that creates a better arrangement.
So, give all you can, and you will be rewarded.

Keep an open heart to those whom would know you,
For there is hope for everyone to find their perfect mate.
Even those of you which do not hold with the romantic notions of flowers and candlelight,
There are your opposite partners in the world, somewhere.

March 15th, 1993

Commence with an attraction, one for the other,
And build upon a foundation of compassion and understanding.
These will give you ample grounds to create a bond that will last.
But, there is no guaranteed formula that will force a relationship.

Having mutual interests helps with almost every new beginning between a man and woman,
Except when their personalities clash, and then there may be no hope for them becoming a couple.
Give what you can to the budding promise of Love,
But don't over do what comes, because if it is meant to be, it will be.

When all has been done that safely may,
Then it can be worthwhile if you should stay together.
But, if you drift apart, don't blame one and the other,
Because it was probably just not meant to be.

There are many opportunities for everyone to find the right mate,
And you must not give up hope because of past failures.
Be persistent in your efforts to overcome all obstacles.
The goal, marriage, is the only worthwhile method of living between man and woman.

March 15th, 1993
(Part B)

Be patient with those who do not seem to understand even the basic decencies.
They have probably not been exposed to the same manners as you.
And everyone can learn, if given the opportunity.
Plus, you should count it in your favor if you should be able to help another see the light.

Having the gift of being able to teach, and not using it,
Should be counted as on of the unforgivable sins against Mankind.
Because there are so few people that can honestly instruct others,
And have those others' eyes opened to the wonders of learning.

March 15th, 1993
(Part C)

To understand the what and where of a situation between two or more people,
You must first take each side, and attempt to fathom them.
Then you just may have a chance to act as a good mediator of any dispute.
The fallacy is when you inject your own opinions before careful consideration of the already disputing parties.

Giving all sides an equal opportunity to express their views,
Will give better form to those views and a chance for the opposition to comprehend the others opinions.
There is no fault in the stating of the premises more than once,
Because when there is any uncertainty, that is where hostility breaks the peaceful realm of negotiation.

There may well be those disputes which will have no workable solution.
In those instances one must give a little of what they wanted, and work a compromise.
The only victor in open hostilities being the makers of ordinance, and those whom have invested in same.
Do not fall victim to the Robber Barrens of the present day.

The people with the most to loose are the ones which will loose their freedom and lives in open hostilities.
And all those which instigated the affront, shall only profit by others' suffering.
Since the world began, a few selfish people have usually had their way;
And because of this repeating of history, we suffer as a species, and there is continued strife among nations and people.

March 16th, 1993

Coming to understand the meaning of responsibility for your actions,
Does things to your feelings towards each other and friends.
There are no easy answers for those of us which do not want them,
And when the way seems smooth, beware of all that may hinder you.

When the time comes for us to accept what comes our way,
Do not let anyone stand in the way of the progress that will help you along the path.
There may be some semi-rough times ahead,
But with Love and understanding, all is possible.

Be of good spirits when taking on new challenges in the game of life,
And do not let anyone give you false hope for a tomorrow that may not be.
Just because it seems the right thing to do,
Do not let the opinion of anyone else guide you to a wrong answer.

If there is no way that anyone else may have a voice in your decision,
Then there should be no outside influence upon your conclusions.
All things being equal among yourselves,
You should enjoy what you have, when you have it.

March 16th, 1993
(Part B)

The major desire of all thinking people,
Seems to be centered, if the thinking person is also completely logical, in the needs of others.
Because the self centered person cannot manage his affairs with others very well,
And there are no excuses rendered of given for selfish people.

Having the correct frame of mind for all of the interplay between you and others,
Takes a special type of attitude toward life and people.
Compromising and adapting is the key to most successful people,
And the ones that cannot understand this, are most typically bitter and selfish people.

Have trust and faith in yourself and those around you.
There is little hope of ever attaining world peace without a beginning of some sort,
And there is no better place to start, than with yourself.
So, when reading the evening news or viewing it, think what you could do to change the outcomes on some of those depressing stories.

Have no fear of being misunderstood when attempting to correct some injustice.
For, even if you are, at least you will know that you have made the effort in good faith.
Release your inhibitions about how you might appear in the eyes of others,
And give of yourself to those you judge in true need; you will not regret it.

March 17th, 1993

Having finally gotten what you wanted in life,
And not realizing that it is really not what you needed,
May give you happiness for a time, and all could be well.
But if comprehension dawns, learn to accept the things that you have as gifts should be.

Love, a wondrous emotion, and nothing to be trifled with,
Especially when there is no other substitute for this feeling when shared.
And, although rare, Love is often shared by couples,
Whether they have known each other for decades or only weeks.

Use your God given intelligence to make a choice,
Between giving yourself or withholding from another.
There are only so many chances for True Love to blossom,
So, have a care that you don't let it slip from your grasp, when you finally get a handle on it.

March 17th, 1993
(Part B)

Taking from friends and family is a full time occupation for some,
There are those who feel they deserve all they can persuade others out of.
Then there are those who feel that whatever they can do to make life easier and better for you, they will do,
And they are the ones that make life more enjoyable for us all.

March 20th, 1993

On a Saturday morning of a retreat to the past in life style,
There comes a time when you should think of being prepared for further adventure.
There might be something that has slipped beyond your grasp in measured time,
That may come back to you in future, with a little help from family.

Give yourself a chance to appreciate what you have,
Because there may not be that much that others may think you understand,
Give all hope of obstinacy away,
And you will have a better time with yourself and everyone else.

March 22nd, 1993

A home of your own, whether it be luxurious or mundane,
Gives a couple or single person reason to be proud of what has conspired to accomplish this feat.
Making a house, apartment, or condo a home is all the special little extras,
And nothing replaces the feelings shared by a couple of excitement and anticipation of making a house into a home.

The necessities of life give one reason to work at what will supply us with these.
Additionally, we often wonder why there is not the pleasure of enjoying what we have accomplished.
People that dread work are missing the great opportunities which may arise,
From feelings of a job well done, and what one person can accomplish in life.

When you put these together,
You will find that you cannot have one without the other.
And when you have someone to share these tribulations with,
All the better for you both, and everyone around you.

March 22nd, 1993
(Part B)

Spring is here, and has arrived after a long winter,
And all of nature's gifts are greatly appreciated by all.
The wonders of fresh cut grass and flowers in bloom,
Are something that heralds every spring and summer for the South.

Having someone to share the cycles of the seasons with,
Is a wondrous miracle that should not be taken for granted.
Not appreciating all that the other does for you
Is a sin against yourself as much as against the other.

To My Wife
March 23rd, 1993

Having said most of all there is to say on the subject of Love,
Will never happen in a life time of living a full, rich existence with a partner.
You can never express, verbally, how deep your feelings are, if you are truly in Love.
That is how it should be, between man and woman.

Making the attempt to express you Love to another,
Is a soul searching endeavor that takes thought, understanding, and compassion.
It seems that the more you put into it, the more you have left to say.
Still you really cannot measure up to how you really feel about the light of your life.

The luminous point in my life, is my wife.
I don't know what or where I would be without her,
And I know that I would be much the worse than I am now,
For I would not know any of the many joys of sharing myself with someone whom returned in kind.

There are not many women in this world that have the truly empathic bent, as my loving wife.
She truly cares, not only for me and her children and grandchildren,
But for everyone she meets, and they have the good fortune to bask in her aura of Love.
When this life is done, I look forward to sharing eternity with my soul mate, the Lady of my life.

To a Troubled Lady, and others like her
March 23rd, 1993

Give credit where credit is due,
And do not over emphasize the accomplishments you have aspired to.
Simply because you are who you are, and there is no one else exactly similar,
Don't become prideful, because humility becomes even the greatest of people.

Take care of yourself, and love yourself well.
If you do not, you will not be worth the love of anyone else.
It is true that you may incur the infatuation of many others,
But you will most likely drive them away, because of your self hate.

Hate is but the flip side of love,
And if you do not love yourself, you more than likely hate yourself, to some extent.
That is not healthy, and it will catch up to you eventually.
Be not concerned with the opinions of others about you, you have to live with yourself, not all others.

When being apart and alone seems the best course for you,
Because you don't trust yourself not to hurt another,
Then you know that you do not love yourself, or even respect yourself very much.
It is of no concern how handsome or beautiful you are, because God does not judge beauty on a physical scale.

Do not feel ashamed of yourself for not practicing chastity at all times,
Because the body, in order to stay healthy, must be used in all it's parts.
If luck would have it, you just may find more than simple physical attraction.
When that occurs, you should make an effort to nourish that seed.

If you should find yourself alone, and in need,
Count you true friends by the number that come to your aide.
If they number more than none,
Then you may deem yourself very lucky.

March 23rd, 1993
(Part B)

Arriving at a point in life where what matters most is the people involved with you,
And no longer caring so much for material possessions,
You might find it a less stressful existence than you have known before.
No longer will money make that much difference to you, and your friends will number more than you might easily count.

The idealistic is hard to live by in any day and time,
But it is worth working at for all of us.
For the need has not been more evident than it is now that we all put aside our petty squabbles,
And try to make this world a little better place for everyone.

March 24th, 1993

Homemaking should be an occupation shared by a couple and family,
There should be no separation of responsibilities between the couple.
Ideally, all should share in the joys of preparing a house as a home,
And it should be something that keeps all parties involved.

Give what you can to the effort of togetherness in making a home,
And you shall be repaid ten fold with praise from all.
It is difficult to prepare a house for the living which must take place there.
Perhaps, if you all give it your best shot, you shall have something everyone may be proud of.

Think of what it will mean to you to have a place that can be called yours,
And never try to postpone the work which needs to go into the effort.
Just because there are no ground rules, do not think you may simply jump in and go.
There needs to be order to what you do, even if chaotic at times.

March 24th, 1993
(Part B)

Take care in your dealings with people,
Whether casual acquaintances or long time friends.
You may find both categories to be helpful, or a hindrance if you disregard their feelings.
Do not be surprised if nothing comes from resources you just thought were a sure thing, if you treat others as insignificant to your needs.

All people have the need to feel they are important to someone,
And there may be no better chance for gaining their support, than making them feel that way.
Be a sensitive individual when it comes to your dealings with others,
Because there is no reason not to, and it will only benefit you in the long run.

March 25th, 1993

All things that come to you through your labor are deserved,
Even if they seem to be extravagant in nature, you should accept what is earned.
Do not think that just because you have more than most, that it is undeserved,
Because there comes a time that gives meaning to the words of many about only having what is rightfully yours.

Of all the beginnings that we attempt,
The start of a budding relationship is the most important.
Do not think that there is a substitute for a spouse,
Because there surely is not, even if you are not legally bound, no person is whole without a partner for life.

Take care of yourself, and you will find that there is hope,
And the greatest hope of all lies in the hearts of others that you touch.
When finding out about your frailties, think of how they affect others.
You might discover that they are not as bad as you thought at first.

Discovery of self can be a rewarding experience,
Even if you are not a saint in your own eyes, you may be in another persons'.
Believe what you will about the world at large,
But it is sometimes a forgiving place, when taken in the right manor.

March 26th, 1993

Of all the possibilities involved in discovering who you really are,
There is no better judge as to which course to take than yourself.
Give consideration to other people in your life,
But the final decision of what you will be is yours.

Do not leave work half done, or things unsaid that need saying.
Those are the types of things that make for regrets,
And no one needs any more guilt over things left undone.
So, be as through as possible when planning projects and relations with others.

Have the audacity to discover for yourself what is good and bad,
And let no one else make up your mind for you.
If you have doubts or questions, ask for advice,
But do not take everything you hear for the gospel.

Take advantage of your youth to the fullest extent you can,
For youth is a fleeting thing, that will not stay with anyone forever.
Be careful in what you aspire to accomplish in life,
Because there are some things better left undone and words better off not spoken.

March 26th, 1993
(Part B)

Partake of all the pleasures which you may decently have access.
But do not rule out pleasures that you think improper simply because you haven't tried them.
Think what it is you are doing in respect to others,
For nothing can be good if it harms someone else.

Have a care for some of the things that you would like to have happen,
Because those things might prove not only harmful to you, but to others.
Simply because something seems to be a good idea at the time,
Doesn't necessarily mean that it will stand the test of time.

Be retrospective in your outlook on life,
And be assured that there will not be the necessity of boredom for long.
There is always some little quirk of nature that will pique your fancy,
And then you rediscover why you are here.

Give thought to the welfare of others,
But not to the extent of harming your own.
And think not on how much you may do for yourself,
Temper self indulgence with moderation, and do not over indulge others, either.

March 28th, 1993

Guidance is something we all may need more than once in our lifetime.
There aren't any sure fire methods of obtaining the correct advice when needed.
Giving advice is simple, but giving good advice is not,
And learning to differentiate the two is maturing.

March 29th, 1993

Having a place that may be deemed Home,
Is a special thing which raises feelings in us all of comfort and security.
There is no better feeling than to share a home with your spouse and family.
You won't find that feeling anywhere, or with anyone else.

Think of how you might achieve the comfort factor given by a home of your own,
And think not of how you might otherwise garner satisfaction.
Other types of satisfaction are not quite as nice,
And, although there are other kinds of pleasures, nothing beats a home, made together with a family.

Giving all that you have in order to produce what you can,
And making something lasting out of the fabric of Love between you and your spouse,
Is what I call making a home for all to share.
Giving that little bit extra, makes it even better.

It matters not how luxurious your surroundings may be,
So long as you share what you have with as many as possible,
And the warmth of you Love keeps everyone in comfort.
Believe what you will, there is no other feelings that mean so much as Love of Home and family and friends.

March 29th, 1993
(Part B)

Exuding the feeling of togetherness between a man and a woman,
Is something called Love, and should be shared with everyone possible.
Just the simple sharing will give to all a good, warm glow that might be carried into their lives,
And, who knows, it just may spread around the globe.

Being selfish with you Love, is not really what it is about,
And cannot truly be Love in the best sense.
It is something that is more closely attuned with greed, than Love,
Because if there is true love, you want everyone to share in it.

All feelings of mistrust should be abolished between a loving couple,
And only the purest of light should be allowed to shine on them.
Have no thoughts of jealousy or ownership of your lover,
Because these are childish things that no adult should indulge in.

Give hope to all those less fortunate than yourself,
That they too may find true love in this sometimes hard world.
There is someone out there for everyone,
But you must be open to them in order to find what it is you seek.

March 31st, 1993

New beginnings commence in our lives with regularity that astonishes most,
And there should be no reason for such amazement at something so fundamental to life.
Having a fresh start everyday, you should be thankful for what you have begun,
And not dwell over much on what is past.

April 2nd, 1993

Upon completion of what is thought to be the last big move in your life,
You should stop and consider what it is that you have moved from.
If what you are moving to is truly worth what has had to be sacrificed,
Then the move was correct.

There are not many people that enjoy moving so much when it is forced upon them.
It is always a consummate hassle when it has to all be accomplished in so short a time.
If it can be spread out over some number of days, then it is easier.
When preparation of the destination has been accomplished beforehand, it makes it even easier.

Have a hope of finding your perfect home or home site,
And be not discouraged at looking for your place in the world,
Because there is a place for us all that we may truly be comfortable with,
Even if it costs us an arm and a leg, it is worth it for the pleasure of having a home of our own.

April 3rd, 1993

Being in the home of your dreams,
Whether or not it is a place or a state of mind,
Brings all the joys of togetherness to focus.
Because a home is where you have family and loved ones.

Think of all the wonderful aspects of life that the homeless of the world must endure without.
A shelter is one of the basic needs of all living beings,
And to deprive even one person of a home is a sin.
If there were a way not to, and there is if we will search our souls for a method, everyone should be provided with a home.

When the time of judgment for everyone on earth has come,
Where will you stand in relation to the Lord and how He lived His life on earth?
There may be no one day where everyone goes before the second coming,
But for each individual, there will surely be a judgment that he or she will have to spend eternity with.

Attempt to analyze yourself enough to the point where you may make judgment upon yourself,
And if the judgment is not favorable, then change what you judge is not good.
Because if you only have to answer to your conscience, that should be enough of a persuader to live your life more kindly toward others.
The old "Golden Rule" is applicable and a logical way of living anyone's life.

April 4th, 1993

Upon most Sunday mornings in this world of strife and turmoil,
You will find a little peace in the air that might not be broken all day long.
That is not to say that ii will not be, but that if the harmony is broken, it is always a shame.
There will always be the prospect of another Sunday at the beginning of the next week.

Take this opportunity to give thanks to whatever Lord or God you worship for all that you have,
And you will not be far wrong if you thank those closest to you for their help and friendship.
Most people do not believe that what they have, they have only by the grace of God,
But if it were not for Him, none of us would have anything.

Being in the position of being able to help your fellow man with his problems, ,
And taking the opportunity to do so, is, perhaps, the most praiseworthy of all humanitarian acts.
Everyone should appreciate a truly good person,
And not take advantage of that person to the extent of turning him away from humanity.

Being a person of a caring and responsible disposition,
And being taken advantage of, will not give rise to any thought of retaliation.
That means that you would have stooped to the level of meanness and cruelty of your adversary.
Be the same toward all, and do not think that if taken for granted by some, that all will do so.

April 5th, 1993

The most beautiful wife in the world lives with me.
She has the most delightful children and grandchildren that I have ever had the good fortune to meet.
There are no reservations as to whether or not she will remain my best girl,
Because she feels the same about me as I do about her.

My wife and I have been building our lives around the hope of finding each other.
We did so on June 25th, 1991 at the restaurant at the "High Noon Saloon".
When you find someone so perfect for you that words cannot express your emotions,
Then more is the shame if you let that someone slip away.

We both feel that we have found the perfect mate in one and the other.
I cannot think of anything else that I could wish for in a spouse.
When the time of our lives arrives for us to consolidate our feelings and thoughts;
That time will be an ongoing recompense with each other, and is continually in the now.

I feel as if my whole life has been spent in preparation for meeting and wedding my wife.
There could not be a more perfect match of two kindred spirits on this earth.
Perhaps there have been others who have felt toward each other the way we do;
But I can only speak from personal experience that there could only be a few so lucky.

April 5th, 1993
(Part B)

Upon coming of maturity in your dealings with the opposite sex,
You will come to understand that everyone is desperately seeking the same thing, Love.
No matter what people say or how they act toward each other, it all stems from their search for someone to care for and bared for by.
When two people do finally find each other, that can be the most beautiful thing in the world.

Have the courage to open yourself to people,
Because if you do not, you will never make that connection with the perfect mate for you.
Even if you get hurt, it is better to have some feeling than to hide yourself away.
Never think that by secluding yourself you have solved your problem, that is only creating another.

If there comes a time when you feel that life has passed you by,
Realize what it is that has come from your not allowing others into your heart.
Take action to change those circumstances to your own favor.
Don't become a bitter and lonely person, there is no need for that.

Simply open yourself to what comes your way,
You will find that almost everyone you meet will like and appreciate you;
Even if some do not, you will find that those are the ones who have secluded themselves behind walls.
All you can do is offer yourself as an example of what it is to be open to the world.

April 6th, 1993

Having friends is a lot better than having money in the bank,
When you are sad or lonely, you can always call on a friend to break the spell.
The type of friend that is always there when you truly need them,
Is a person so rare and fine, that they should truly be cherished throughout your life.

If you think that you are better off without the comfort of friends and family,
And that money will see you through all of life's hardships,
You have missed the boat somewhere along the dock.
Money will not make you laugh or talk to you when you need it.

Gold will get you the material possessions that are needed to live in comfort,
But there must be no substitution of Gold for people in your life.
Think what it would be like to have all the money you ever dreamed of,
And not to have one single person that would call you friend.

The contemplation of the wealthy is mostly concerned with how to make more or hoard what they have.
This is the beginning of the downfall of all who act this way;
They are the most assuredly lonely people that you will ever meet.
You will hardly ever see them smile at the antics of children.

Dedicated to a businessman I knew
April 6th, 1993

Becoming one with another, even only physically, leads to sharing things that everyone should long for.
There is no finer expression of your love for each other, than joining your fate together as one.
Of all the people in this world that have ever become as one, yours is the most important.
Trust everyone as if that person could become your friend or mate, and you will not go wrong in this life.

All of the dreams of people throughout time have mostly concerned themselves with happiness.
The only true happiness is the kind shared by two or more.
A selfish person is never truly happy,
Because he is always fearful of someone taking or obtaining something he has or wants.

Give consideration to the aspect of falling into the crevice of despair caused by greed.
There has never been a good person that lived his entire life obtaining possessions and wealth for their own sake,
And if you do fall into that trap, then the world will pity you more than respect you.
Most people with common sense will realize what parts of your humanity you must have given up.

There could be hope for even the vilest of misers,
But that hope lies within that person's mind and soul.
There is nothing that may be done to obtain the wealth of spirit,
That does not include a love of self and your fellow humans.

April 7th, 1993

When all around you seems dim and bleak,
There could be a supposition of depression which has fallen over your countenance.
The only method to disavow yourself of this, is to force yourself into action.
It is hard to realize that everyone, not just you, has trouble at some time or another.

Give thought to others less fortunate than yourself,
That have not even the food needed to sustain a healthy body.
These are becoming more and more prevalent all over the globe, instead of fewer.
There is enough food to feed these people, but still they starve.

In the best of all possible worlds,
There would be no want on the part of any;
And everyone would be at least as happy as could be expected.
This would be a somewhat boring world, and I wish for it.

April 7th, 1993
(Part B)

There seems no end to what should be done with regard to how your time is spent
In making your dwelling into a home that all can see is warm and comfortable.
When the time is spent in honest endeavor to better your surroundings and life,
Then you have not wasted any, and the fruits of your labor should be evident to all.

Give up the notion that you live apart from all in the world.
Everyone is connected in one form or another throughout the world.
There is truth to the saying: "No man is an island";
Because everyone needs someone to hitch their wagon for.

Be of peaceful mind when it comes to your dealings with others,
And do not underestimate the ability of others on your behalf.
There are no guarantees as far as life's trials are concerned,
And the only way to overcome, is to put your fate, with hard work, into faith and Love.

April 7th, 1993
(Part C)

Be of contented mind when dealing with life's problems,
And have no disquieting thoughts as concerned with interaction with others.
Do not believe what has gone before will of necessity have great impact on the present,
Because everything in the past will not necessarily burden the future.

Have confidence in your abilities to handle what comes your way,
And do not feel that just because you are crest fallen at one point,
That this will continue into your future.
Everyday brings new opportunities to handle things a little differently.

Be not over concerned with how others affect your being happy.
They have influence, but you are the final factor in determining your state of mind.
Have the good sense to not let others effect a detrimental change;
And be not to empathetic to other peoples problems that it damages you.

April 7th, 1993
(Part D)

Realization of errors, both past and present,
Leads one to doubts that have no place in the confident.
In order to discontinue mistakes, you must have confidence.
This comes from within, but it helps if the powers that be have some in you, also.

Noting that errors beget errors,
And nothing that may be done will erase those already past,
You should look forward to establishing something for yourself other than a history of errors.
Be pleased with who you are and what you do, for you must live with these.

Care should be taken in how you perform at the behest of others,
Because only you may fairly determine the quality of your work.
Above all there should only be those things passed on which will last.
Do not think that whatever you do is all right, unless you would be satisfied with the product for yourself.

April 8th, 1993

The occurrences in life which take the most time are sometimes those which we care most about.
These are mostly involved with family and friends.
It is never a waste of time to include a benediction for a friend,
Because there is no finer person than one whose only purpose is to be your friend.

Take the time and effort needed to cultivate friends whenever possible,
And you will not drift far from the mark of humanitarian action.
For anything you do will seem better if it involves friendship.
There are not many people that we can truly name as our friends, so cherish those you have.

Give all that you can to those in need,
For there is no telling when you might also be in need.
Do not believe that people's misfortunes are all their own doing;
Because, often times, that is only a small portion of their problem.

There are often times when we would wish for the comfort of children,
And the joys experienced by these miniature people.
But those times are past for most of us,
And only the escapists still cling to childish ways.

April 8th, 1993
(Part B)

When you come to the realization that not all in this world can be taken at face value,
And it seems that the things you depended upon most, always being the same, change,
You have come to understand the meaning of life as an ever changing environment.
Someday you will also learn how to persuade the fates to let you have a little consistency in some of your life.

April 8th, 1993
(Part C)

Working towards a goal of never having to want for anything again
Is what we all do with our lives in the work place.
There is no other reason to work, unless we truly enjoy that pastime.
If you are one of those, count yourself lucky.

Give up all pretense of not having fun in life,
Because a person that has no fun cannot truly be totally human.
Just because there does not seem to be as much opportunity for pleasure,
Does not mean that pleasures are all past for you.

Ponder how this world would get along without all the variety of people,
And you would come close to understanding what being a part of the scheme of life is about.
There may or may not be a great plan for us,
But, even if not, the experience we garner here will stand us in good stead.

April 11th, 1993

Coming of age on an Easter Sunday will bring with it joy and longing.
For there aren't many that ever mature enough to prosper well into the future.
Those that do not become involved in a lot of different aspects of life,
Are those that have a very narrow view of the world as it should be.

Given that a lot of people feel exposed and insecure about sharing themselves with others,
It is getting harder every year to find those who share even a little kindness.
Do not think that they are impossible to find,
For they are still out there in the world, you simply must look harder.

Be of simple disposition when it comes to dealing with people,
And you will be much happier when they perform unexpectedly well.
Do not bother yourself with the errors made by others,
For you can only truly control your own.

April 12th, 1993

Loving the beauty of life, and how it is lived with someone very special,
Is what the true meaning of life is all about;
And should be the goal of every feeling human now on this earth.
There are not so few of these couples as might be supposed.

The beginning of finding a person of the caliber that will fill the gaps in your life is the hardest part;
But once you have gotten past that start, the rest is simply a matter of staying open to the prospects.
Be of quiet mind and let the simple pleasures bring you joy.
All these will make you a much better prospect in yourself.

The hope of bringing to yourself the pleasures of Love, and having someone that cares in the same way,
Could be the simplest of all possible chores in life.
Most people want to make it the most difficult,
And these are the people that fight the natural flow of nature.

When you have finally found the mate that you have been either actively or passively seeking,
You will understand what it is that makes life the most beautiful experience.
You will no longer turn up your nose at all the poets and songwriters speaking of Love,
For you will have joined their ranks.

April 13th, 1993

Begin the attempt to comfort yourself with the thought that all is well,
And have no fear of what might transpire in the future to upset the apple cart.
Because the future is assured if the present is taken care of.
Do not let symbolism enter into the equation of what you need for happiness.

Give up the notion that material possessions will bring happiness,
And the whole world will not be able to take it away from you.
Don't think that material things are of necessity bad,
They just do not mean very much in the scheme of life.

Have the maturity to realize that although you might long for more than you have,
You will not be happy just because you have obtained them.
This has never been a key to Heaven,
And will not even buy very much happiness on Earth.

April 14th, 1993

The greatest hope of all of us sharing this earthly coil of flesh,
Is that we will find true happiness with the miracle of a partner to share our dreams with.
There may be some solitary endeavors to which you might find some measure of gladness,
But they are made all the more meaningful when there is someone there to do them for.

All the world over you will find the same search for happiness occupying mankind,
And it doesn't matter what part of the globe you happen to be in,
People are pretty much the same the world over in that regard.
Try to understand that much of the world's unease occurs when people in power become to greedy for what they think they need.

If you should ever become so disgusted with the world that you don't want any part of it,
Take time to appreciate at least yourself and your own caring nature.
Realize that the world needs more people such as you.
There just may be some redeeming qualities in the world that you could think of.

April 15th, 1993

When there is no other person in your life to share your victories or defeats,
And to comfort you in times of temporary failure,
It can be a very lonely life you lead.
To rectify this state of affairs, should be your only goal.

For those of us that share this thing called life with a partner,
There can never be much thought of not having someone there when needed most.
There might be times when we are not totally in tune,
But these are fewer and fewer as time goes on.

Give up the notion that you can do just as well on your own without a spouse,
Because that is not how the good Lord intended us to live.
It is a mean and lonely life without someone there for you.
So, do not think that just because you are seemingly happy alone, that it is all the same.

April 15th, 1993
(Part B)

Giving to the obvious what has been hidden from you,
Will bring anger to some and acceptance to others.
There could be explanations as to why the blatant truth has eluded you,
Such as, you were stuck with an unreasoning outlook on others and life
in general.

The prospect of not knowing which way to turn,
And having to many options and opinions offered to guide you,
Bring its' own type of schizophrenic haziness to your mind.
Unless you take them slowly, and one at a time.

Do not be misguided by a seemingly thoughtless response.
Those are the type that most others will not have qualms about offering.
If they are worthy of second consideration,
You will know by the way the words strike you, and how much thought
went into them.

April 16th, 1993

Become one with the person you care most about,
Whether it be yourself or another, you must first Love yourself.
Do not think that the place or time is not yet right,
For if you think over much about propriety you will never take the first step.

Feel what you are best able to in regard to your neighbor,
But do not let wantonness enter into your mind.
There are no substitutes for wholesome Love of they neighbor,
And that is one of the commandments set forth to live by.

All of the wanderings of mind and body have to do with finding your place in the world,
And when you truly feel that you place is secure,
You must not question why this is so.
That questioning may bring doubts that will hinder instead of help you.

April 16th, 1993
(Part B)

Understanding why you behave the way you do is the essence of becoming adult.
For all past failures to live up to your own expectations,
You will need to forgive yourself.
This will help to make you the type of person who is not critical and judgmental of others, as well.

The worse form of religion as practiced by some, is of the type that truly believes theirs is the only true path to the Lord.
There are so many of these that summarily pass judgment on others,
That if any one were truly correct, then almost the whole of humanity would be condemned.
This seems a very unlikely method for the Lord to practice His beliefs, and I do not think He said anything in His teachings that give credence, above others, to any one path.

Hope was and is given by the Lord to all that would believe in Him.
There is no other path that leads to Heaven that does not have this as a cornerstone.
Let the fanatics practice what they will,
For some people need to feel that they have a secret that no outsiders will be able to share.

April 18th, 1993

Upon discovering what you are truly meant to do in life,
You should set about to conquer all obstacles in your path to achieve that goal.
There should be nothing that may stand in your way for long,
And, in the spirit of humanity, there should be no one that would want to stop you.

Because all of us are on a life time quest for what we truly like to do,
And where we want to live our lives and with whom,
We should not stop anyone else from trying to do the same.
We will be happier if we can help someone else along the way, and our path will be made easier.

Do not believe that you can ride rough shod over obstacles,
Because that will not work for very long with people in general.
It never works well with family.
You will be more satisfied if you are generous and kind, than gruff and stingy.

Of all the people that we meet in this joint journey through life,
The ones we remember most are those that affect us either detrimentally or beneficially.
The ones that will live in our fondest memories are those that have given more than they have received.
Be as generous as possible, for it will be returned to you a thousand fold.

April 19th, 1993

Going about your business everyday,
With only the thought of a loving spouse and comfortable home to see you through,
Has all the benefits of life that anyone could hope to gain.
Whether they were wealthy with gold or friends and family.

Give credit to those millions of people that find joy in all the simple pleasures of life,
And do not have to succumb to the pressures that life seems so prone to.
These are those people that take what comes and go on their way,
With a smile for those they pass and good feelings left with them for their efforts.

Do not think that all the people of the world are as obtuse as most seem to be.
Those which do not think that anyone else is important,
And those that forget that their problems and victories are not the sum total of existence.
There are those wonderful, wholesome and friendly people that are willing to lend a hand when needed.

They are not so many as was once the case,
Because of all the abusive people that have taken advantage of them.
Some of those that would be good Samaritans, have ceased,
And the others are guarded, but there are still some around.

April 20th, 1993

The wonderful aspect of having a new day in which to perform your own type of miracle,
That of loving someone so wonderful as my soul mate, my wife.
There are not quite so many of these wonderful people as we would all wish,
But everyone has the potential to be one, if they would only let themselves.

When I contemplate what life would be like without my wonderful wife,
I can only think of the loneliness and despair that I experienced when we did not have each other.
We both know that, no matter what comes our way, we will always have each other.
This is all we truly need to be happy, and you will find the same is true for you.

When the time comes for you to find someone to share your life with,
Do not be so obstinate that you let all pass you by without even a hope.
There is the possibility that the one you let slip by would have been the one for you.
Be positive that you will make a happy life for you both, and it will happen.

There is no obstacle that can stand in the way for long against true Love.
All that Love implies means that whatever or whoever would oppose it, doesn't stand a chance.
And those that think they can abuse another persons love, are only fooling themselves,
For they are truly only hurting themselves more than they will ever hurt a loving person.

Give thought to what life is like alone,
And you will realize that this is no way to live.
Even if you believe you have all that you will ever need,
Without someone to share it with, you have next to nothing.

April 20th, 1993
(Part B)

Take up the banner of kindness, and be gentle with the ones you love.
The rewards of doing so far out weigh any possible disadvantages.
You will benefit yourself for all of those people will treat you as you do them.
There may be times when it will not be easy, but try anyway.

April 21st, 1993

The best of us do not always act toward others the way we should,
And there is no reason for us to feel badly about temporary lapses.
Just because there may be times when we are not at our best, doesn't mean we are bad,
Only that we aren't having a good day.

Believe what you will about people in general,
There is basic good in everyone.
Even those that have done reprehensible acts against humanity.
They have gone terribly wrong due to mental or physical abuse, and they can change.

There are those that you would not want to be caught in an alley with,
And these need the most help in overcoming their predisposition toward violence.
Just because they are sometimes violent, does not mean that they have always been so.
They must be caught up in a stage of development that is more like a four your old, than a reasoning adult.

April 22nd, 1993

Understanding that there is a time and place for all of your discovery and wonder of Love,
Comes to us all in our lives if we are going to truly live them.
There might be some cases of people that come to this understanding early in life,
And others that will not have the light dawn on them until much latter.

To be among those that will have the best of what life has to offer,
You must first be willing to take a chance on people of short acquaintance with yourself,
And give everyone the benefit of a doubt when it comes to feelings.
There is no better time than the present to start a trusting attitude toward the opposite sex.

Hopefully and faithfully not to many people will hurt you if you open up to them.
There will always be some that will,
But the number that will not is growing as time goes on.
Take the chance, you have nothing to lose but loneliness.

April 22nd, 1993
(Part B)

All of the people that have ever come into contact with those of unreasoning temperament,
Will agree that it is best to simply pass by, and not attempt to argue reason into their thick skulls.
If you can make your point without becoming upset,
Then you have learned one of the great secrets of life as we know it.

Understanding what has gone before to make an obstinate person the way he is,
Gives one better understanding of how to deal with him.
But at times no matter what your understanding, you would like to take a ball peen hammer to the offender's skull.
So, give thanks if no one of your acquaintance classifies you in that category.

April 24th, 1993

There comes a time in everyone's life when having someone to share what comes is all important,
And finding that someone is all that occupies their mind and heart.
Attempting to force the issue with any one person might result from this pursuit,
But that is not the method best suited in matter of Love.

If the spark is there between two people,
Then it must be nurtured by careful attention to romance and practicality.
When it becomes natural to be together and have no inhibitions about yourself,
The match has a chance to go the distance.

Being self involved will no longer be a viable form of personality,
And thinking only of the one you love will seem only natural.
So be of mild temperament when it comes to the opposite sex,
Because the forceful will only beget a mate that is somnolent and meek.

April 25th, 1993

Giving to your lover what is only deserved by her or him,
Has to be one of the qualifications upon any lasting relationship.
To not attempt to please your lover, only makes you a selfish type of lover.
That type of thing has gone the way of the Dodo bird.

Be not humble to the point of complete passivity to your own good points.
Do not underestimate everyone else in your acquaintance;
Because most people will surprise you with the quality of their being,
And with the basic demeanor that they exhibit you might not think of them as being able to understand what makes you tick, but they can.

Go about your business with the hope of not being in the wrong in dealing with people,
And, perhaps, you will bring to yourself a greater benefit of feelings than you thought possible.
Just because there are a lack of the type of feelings you would hope for in your life at the present,
Doesn't mean that it will be a void forever.

Dedicated to a Dancing Teacher & His Partner
April 25th, 1993

Having come full circle back to the beginning of what you had when you both found each other,
you must realize that you really have nothing worth fighting over by yourselves.
If children are a cause, they will eventually grow up, and leave you.
Another lover might be explainable, but if your relationship was of a lasting nature, then another lover would not stand a chance anyway.

The responsibilities that come with parenthood are many and varied, and sometimes seem never ending;
But they do come to an end, and if you have no one to share the remainder of your time with, you will be awfully lonely.
Come to the real world, people take care of people,
Their needs and wants, and all the many aspects and quirks that make everyone tick.
So, do not let pride or jealousy enter into your heart when dealing with your partner in a relationship.

Come to understand that what you do in this world will live beyond your life,
If you made a good person, then you will be remembered, and contrariwise, you will also be remembered.
Do not be one of the lost ones that does not enjoy what life has to offer with relish,
Be consistent with your dealings with others, and be kind.

April 26th, 1993

The best of life happens when there comes to you a person that will accept your love,
And then nothing in the world can come between you if the match is true.
There might be hard times to come, but you will weather them out.
When family and friends can make it even better, that is the icing on the cake.

There might be times when your mind wanders away from you love,
But those are only a natural part of what makes up life as we know it.
And, although we realize that we should not take people for granted, sometimes we do.
So long as we understand that it sometimes happens, we can compensate for it.

Do not think that life will ever be all a rose garden,
With no thorns to prick your fingers.
There are no guarantees that come with birth,
Only the prospect of discovering what best suits you and the one you choose to live your dreams with.

April 27th, 1993

Upon the coming to life of your emotions as concerned with a significant other,
You might have a tendency to be wary, because of past experience.
Do not be so careful that you loose the possibility of finding that heartache with one doesn't mean you will always have that result.
The one you give up on before you start will never break your heart, but you will also never share what lovers do.

Have a open heart to the possibilities that might ensue with each new person you meet,
And an open mind could not hurt over much;
But do not be so changeable that your personality suffers,
Because that is what makes every person that much the better for someone else.

Remember always that no matter what you may think other people's motives are,
Theirs are somewhat similar to your own.
Human nature is somewhat the same in all of us,
At least the ones worthy of consideration in the first place.

There are those people that are all take and no give,
But they will learn that what they get in that manner will never be worth very much.
Because what is not freely given is not worth the damage to you soul that ensues,
And you may not even benefit from whatever comes, for there is always someone else for those people that take from them.

April 30th, 1993

Understanding the nuances of people's quirks of personality,
And being able to relate to them without seeming to give the appearance of being superior,
Is a special talent that only a few possess and fewer use.
It is not quite so difficult to practice this ability, everyone should be able to cultivate it.

Having a good heart and simply treating people the way you would wish to be treated, is a good way to start.
Not forming prior opinions about how you will act and feel toward others helps, too.
there is no one method for handling everyone you come into contact with,
But being yourself and letting what comes to mind be what you relate to them can get you in a little trouble, sometimes.

When dealing with people, be tactful if you can,
Because not everyone is ready for complete honesty.
Those that think they are, may really not be.
It is something that you will have to use your better judgment about with each person you deal with.

April 30th, 1993
(Part B)

Love has been expounded upon by all the poets and songwriters since recorded history began,
And all that has been said about this emotion still falls short of the emotion itself.
There may be other ways to express your love for someone,
But each must put the other above themselves and care more for others more than they did previously.

Being in love and loving someone is by far the best way to go through life.
Not worrying about what may or may not please the other,
Because you both know each other so well that you have gone beyond the hesitation of first encounter.
You should try to find someone with whom you might share yourself with, for there is no other feeling quite so grand as when shared.

It has been said that nothing worth while is ever very easy,
But loving someone special is quite the easiest thing in the world;
Especially when that other loves you equally.
The whole of existence is made so much more illuminating, when there is a partnership upon which to draw the light of understanding.

May 1st, 1993

Coming to the realization of all the mistakes made in the past by errors in judgment,
Brings with it a maturity and feelings of guilt that will make you a better person.
The trick is to let yourself be forgiven, and try not to repeat what has gone before.
Even though there are not many repetitions of past misjudgments, do not think that you will never make mistakes again.

May 2nd, 1993

Early on a Sunday morning in the spring of the year,
Most people are still wondering why this type of climate cannot be year round.
It is very conducive to good feelings and warmth of both weather and love.
No matter what else may be said of spring, it is a time of renewal and love.

All people around the globe will agree to the one truth that spring and early fall are perhaps the best times of year.
The winter is to cold, and the summer is sometimes to hot,
But spring and early fall has the temperature in just the right spot to let us enjoy the outside.
It also lets us enjoy the inside more, because of the feelings shared by all.

Having the comfort of a relationship which has blossomed into something that you know will last,
And still contains the excitement that you would associate with a new beginning each day,
Is the epitome of what spring is, and a good relationship should be.
Everybody should have this great feeling which is only given by shared love.

May 2nd, 1993
(Part B)

Coming to understand that the only true method for living life to the fullest,
Is the shared life with someone that likes the same things you do,
And cares about you the way you care about them, which is more than you care for yourself.
This is what makes everything in the world more tolerable, and helps us to understand people better.

Just for the reality that we each must face each day,
We all need a retreat to the beauty contained in our loved ones faces.
Nothing will ever replace the feeling we have when we discover each other anew.
That feeling of first encounter and consummation of love for each and the other.

Give up the attitude that you must take what you want or not get anything;
For this is the wrong attitude to assume if you hope to ever truly beget the type of love that will last forever.
The kind of people you encounter with this attitude will only bring you more grief than you already must experience,
And no amount of self justification will make up for the time lost and damage to your soul.

May 4th, 1993

The spring brings with it the sun and warmth, along with some rain and showers,
And both are needed to renew the earth with plants and trees in bloom and leaf.
The time of year is also ripe for the blooming of love and romanticism;
So, do not let the moment escape you before fall's first frost overtakes the earth.

Happening to chance upon a person that could be the one,
And letting the opportunity for love slip by,
Is something that we have all been guilty of in times past.
There is always tomorrow and today to correct this slight.

Be of gentle disposition in regard to all you meet,
For there is no telling who might be of consolation to you;
And who might also be the one for which everyone is looking.
Do not believe that all people are the same, for each has something different to offer.

May 5th, 1993

Being of a receptive nature to any and all that may come your way,
Has it's advantages in that you will not miss out on many opportunities for friendship and enlightenment.
There is the danger of becoming overloaded with people and things that have little substance,
And, although it should not harm you, I doubt that that is always the case.

Moderation in the concepts and new acquaintances that you encounter,
Should be the rule to being a well rounded individual.
Do not let new concepts throw you for a loss of your own values,
Because without them, you become what can only be someone to pity.

May 6th, 1993

Do nothing which will give rise to the seed of doubt in your mind,
About anything that has real meaning or even if it is trivial.
There are corners of perception which are not wholly intended to be explored,
So, have confidence in what you do and what you feel to be constant.

May 7th, 1993

Contemplation leads to some form of action,
Whether it be the action of deciding to do nothing, or to attempt a change.
Leading in the forefront of action to take against mediocrity and boredom,
Is any action at all that does not involve doing nothing.

Be a person of action, especially when it comes to relationships,
Because if you wait for a relationship to happen to you,
You will find that it hardly ever will come your way.
So, take positive action to change whatever it is that holds you back, and truly experience life and love.

May 11th, 1993

The shear joy of being in love with the perfect woman is what every man wishes to experience,
But only a few seem to have the chance.
And every woman would love to have the opportunity to love the perfect man.
There are those perfect people out there for everyone, you simply must find them.

Of all the women I have ever known, only my Lovely wife has given me hope, love and a perfect match.
She has let me know that there is a match for each and every person on this earth, by being my perfect mate.
I simply know that all do, and will have the chance to find someone that is especially for them.
Give to the person you find all that you possibly may, because that is partially what love is about.

The wonder of each day, and the surprising things that she does for me,
Makes me realize all the pleasures that anyone could ever hope to experience.
There are no words that do justice to the way I feel about the wedded bliss that is ours;
And I truly hope that all on the planet will find this happiness with someone else.

May 12th, 1993

The greatest illness in the world today is apathy.
There are no substitutes for caring and participating in the system.
All those which choose not to, have no right to complain about it.
So, whether you are right or wrong in your stand, at least have one.

May 17th, 1993

The failure of most people to understand the basic rules for living with others, leaves me in a quandary;

Whether or not to enlighten people or simply leave them in ignorance.

You would think that everyone would like to be able to associate their aspirations with others,

But some people simply do not understand that the simplest and best rule is the "Golden Rule".

May 18th, 1993

Becoming all that you are capable of is one of the hardest and easiest things in life,
There are guideposts that will assist you on your path.
Many people will offer advice and console that may help.
The final determination of what you accomplish is almost entirely up to you, though.

The prospect of having all that you desire from life,
Should give one the incentive to work hard at becoming whatever one is most suited for.
Even if there are some false starts along the way,
You should not give in to despair for long, because with persistence you will eventually win through.

It matter little what goals you have set,
Just so long as you reach the ones that are important to you.
The goals that involve assisting others with theirs',
Are the most important for a caring individual to obtain.

May 19th, 1993

Beginning with the idea of having someone to share with,
And progressing to the point of taking action to find that person,
Requires a leap of faith in humanity in general, and the one you choose in particular.
Do not be despondent if at first or second attempt the results are not as hoped.

No matter how long the period before you find that special someone,
The trials and tribulations encountered will have been worth it.
So, take heart that with persistence everyone will find what they search for;
Because no matter how many false starts, the budding of love is there for everyone.

May 20th, 1993

Hope for a better chance to improve your lot,
And work towards that goal with consideration to others,
For you will come to the fruition of your labor,
Even if it takes longer than first planned.

Come to life each day with the expectation that you will be surprised,
By either some special something that a person does,
Or by something special that you might spontaneously do for someone.
Be aware that you have little control over events instigated by others, but you can control your reaction to them.

Give thought to what you might do with your life,
To help the general condition of your fellow man,
And look to the future for a better place in which to live.
If everyone is made to share this attitude and outlook on life and people, the world will be a far richer place.

May 20th, 1993
(Part B)

Have love for those whom deserve it,
And pity those which do not.
The not so lovable among us do not understand that no matter their material possessions, they are destitute.
But most people will eventually come to this enlightenment.

The process of fully maturing to a caring and responsible adult,
Is something which takes time and the understanding and nurturing of a lot of people.
Most important among those are the parents,
But do not sell short friends and siblings.

The end result of growing into a person of which respect and love is due,
Is well worth the many arduous missteps that most of us take.
Those who make the journey to that height will attest,
There is no finer feeling of accomplishment in life than that.

May 24th, 1993

When contemplating the beauty of this world,
You should not discount the wonderful aspects of human nature.
All the many things that people are capable of doing for each other,
And all the magical occurrences of people finding each other.

There is no more beautiful specter to behold,
Than the joining of two souls into one.
This happens when two people decide to share all they have with each other.
And is most often culminated in marriage ceremonies.

There could very well be many material beauties that would be worth admiring,
But the beauty found in nature is everlasting, even if cyclical.
The beauty of love shared by two,
Is the most wonderful thing in nature that you will ever behold.

May 24th, 1993
(Part B)

Giving all of your attention to the needs of the past,
Might lead you to overlook the pleasures of the present.
Do not think that all one need to do is take care of basic needs of survival,
For there are more interesting needs that have to do with things and emotions other than those.

The taking of pleasure in simple things that are done for you by someone special,
And those special people that seem always to give of their time and attention,
Are the things and people that make life worth while.
Those people that make those thing happen should be cherished.

May 25th, 1993

Having the instinct to preserve the relationship which flourished in it's youth,
And not regretting a single moment of time spent together,
Is the epitome of what love is about for a couple just starting or those whom have been together for years.
Do not take each other for granted, because that could be the beginning of the end.

Give to your loved one all the time and attention that she needs,
Because if you do not, she will find it somewhere else.
Failing that, she just may become callous to all of your wants and needs.
So, do not fall victim of your own indifference and hurt yourself as well as the one you love.

May 26th, 1993

Participating in the labors of life,
And giving your all to those endeavors,
Will either bring satisfaction or anxiety,
Depending on how well you perform.

Give your all to those important tasks that otherwise would not be done,
And have a care for the people you deal with in handling those tasks.
Have not a worry that you might not perform well,
For if you give your best, you can do no more.

May 27th, 1993

Becoming what is expected of you by yourself,
Is one of the hardest parts of living this life.
It seems that you can never satisfy yourself with simple tasks;
It must always be something more and more demanding.

June 2nd, 1993

The possibilities of finding the right mate in this world are few,
So, if you should be one of the lucky ones that do,
Make every effort to make the relationship work,
Even if there are rough times, weather them out, for you may not ever be so lucky again.

Of all the people that you will meet in your life,
There is only one that will be the perfect match.
Do not settle for less than you deserve,
Because so many have, and lived to regret that mistake.

Be optimistic about your chances of finding your mate,
For you will surely do so, when the time is right.
Hold onto that mate with all your might,
Because you will never find another quite so good for you.

June 2nd, 1993
(Part B)

Giving all you have to give to another worthy of that gift,
Tells all about a person, and about how much the other means.
But not being willing to give even a little of yourself,
Will only leave you a lonely person, with not much hope for remission.

Do not think that all is hopeless in love;
For there is always hope that you will find that perfect someone.
That someone will make the wait and search worthwhile.
Give a little to all you meet, but reserve your all for that special someone.

When wandering through this life with no seeming direction,
Think of all who have done the same and would up with not even a memory left behind.
Be as open as possible to avoid this happenstance,
Because there is no greater waste than a lonely and wasted life.

June 8th, 1993

Being blessed with the foresight and understanding of events that shape your life,
Gives you an advantage over most of the people that are stumbling through this existence.
There can be no goals or dreams that may be realized without this understanding of self.
But, do not despair, for it comes with maturity.

Be not of the type of person that forces his wishes upon others.
This may work in the short run,
But there is no long standing relationship that can endure it.
Do not believe that yours is the only correct answer, there are as many answers as there are people.

Give thought to what others feel and think,
Often it will help with your own problems.
Even if some ideas you come across do not work for you,
There will be others that will.

June 9th, 1993

Having the persistence to stick to a project through all pitfalls,
And never overlooking the ultimate goal,
Takes a special kind of attitude that not many possess.
It you should ever loose sight of your goal, step back and gain your prospective again.

Just because no one else has done something you wish to accomplish,
Does not mean that it cannot be done,
It only means that you will have to break new ground.
So, do not stop before you start, for you will not accomplish anything like that.

The greatest wonder of the world today is the human spirit,
And how it has withstood all attempts to dishearten it.
There are many examples of how people have gone on when seemingly insurmountable obstacles have hindered them.
So, feel not threatened by draw backs to your goal, simply take heart and forge ahead.

Anniversary
June 10th, 1993

Upon the occasion of our first anniversary I would like to say what a great first year,
There has been nothing in my previous experience that could compare.
There is the prospect for many more years of great joy,
And I fervently wish for the number to be many.

All of my life I have been searching for one such as you,
To fill my heart and my time with all the wonders of love.
There is nothing to compare to the love shared by two such as we,
And there quite possibly will not be another love affair to equal ours.

The understanding and compassion that we show each other,
Only makes me wonder how people get along without a spouse.
I can only think tat they must be very lonely,
And that they really do not know what it is that they are missing.

June 10th, 1993
(Part B)

Becoming as one with the one you love is perhaps one of the hardest as well as the easiest aspects of living.
Once accomplished, it is something which will change your whole life,
And there is no better way of living than with someone special.
Even if you have not attained the euphoria of perfect union, it will come if you are persistent.

Looking back on past encounters,
Will surely make you appreciate what you have attained with the present.
Only if your search is at it's end will you truly have realized a dream.
Give up the selfishness that prevents the perfect match, and you will attain the lofty goal.

Finding just one person that suits your needs is a miracle,
And not attempting to do everything you can to stay together is foolish.
Do not let your mate slip through your fingers for any reason.
Only happiness shared is truly meaningful.

June 11th, 1993

The hopes of our future lie within us,
And holding our faith in each other is a major step in realizing those dreams.
When there seems no alternative but to go on with what we started,
That is the culmination of our love for each other coming at last.

Have all the dreams that you can possibly embrace,
For without dreams and imagination we are little better than animals.
There is always the chance that some of those dreams will come true.
Just because all dreams are not fulfilled, do not ever stop dreaming.

Give thought to the aspirations of others,
For no one can make it in this life alone.
Perhaps, if you help others along the way,
You will in turn be helped, and I know that you will be rewarded with a sense of internal warmth.

June 14th, 1993

The realization of a dream is something to look forward to,
And there are still dreams that can be met after one is fulfilled.
Do not look to outside influences to make your dreams come true;
Take it upon yourself to do everything in your power to help the process along.

June 16th, 1993

Of all the possible outcomes in life that you might end up with,
The best is that you will have found the mate best suited for you.
All your dreams together are somehow attainable.
Let no one stand in the way of love and happiness shared by two people.

Have faith in yourself that you will find the answer,
To whatever questions in your life that truly need answering.
Do not worry over much about what others think,
Because the only ones that count are those closest to you.

Bring out the good in yourself and those around you,
You will not find that so difficult a task,
And the rewards are many fold.
Do not despair about things which you cannot change, simply change what wrongs you can.

To My Wife
June 18th, 1993

Looking back on the last year of wedded bliss,
I can only think that all the years to come will be as that one.
There seems that there could only be happiness in our future;
Because we love, honor, and trust each other so completely.

When the great lover's stories are compared,
I can truthfully say that our will be among them.
There couldn't conceivably be any others that are more deserving,
And I know that no others feel for each other more than we.

Giving our all to accommodate each other,
With hardly a thought for the circumstances of outside influence,
And being as one when alone or with others,
Lets us do the near impossible with ease.

There can be no greater joy in life than finding and keeping the love of your life,
And living together as one is perhaps the most wonderful experience that will ever happen to us.
So, be contented with what we now enjoy,
And look forward to all the many years ahead.

July 5th, 1993

When discovering the various aspects of your personality,
Either with someone you love or just an acquaintance,
You should be careful not to over do to the point of complete honesty;
You should not hold back to much either.

Finding the middle ground of what to expose of yourself and what to withhold,
Is perhaps the most difficult part of maturing.
There are not many guidelines that will help in this process,
So, you must use your best judgment, and try to think of these things before you act.

A good upbringing will help in any attempt by you to exhibit your true self,
And it always helps to keep others feelings in mind.
Before all else you must be true to yourself.
There is no time like the present to begin.

July 12th, 1993

The giving of yourself to another is something that should not be done lightly.
When you have found the right person, you will know it;
Do not be overly impatient to simply have someone,
Take the time to make sure it is the right one.

Living with the wrong person for you is perhaps one of the worst sins against yourself and others,
For you have not only harmed yourself, but the one you are with and the one you should be with.
Don't think that just anyone will make you happy forever;
There is only one that can do this for you, and you for them.

July 12th, 1993
(Part B)

The understanding of one's nature is a most difficult concept to grasp in youth.
As the years pass, the concept comes closer to each of us.
For those that never quite have the light dawn upon them,
There is still the hope that they will understand, if someone helps them along.

July 13th, 1993

When the work a day world has got you down,
And there seems no end to the drudgery which is your standard work day,
Think of what it is you are working for and for whom.
There should always be an oasis called home to which you can escape.

If there is no special someone in your life,
And your refuge of home has been more like work,
Then you should make an effort to make everything you must do as interesting as possible.
Be not agitated simply because things do not seem to go your way, it will work out, eventually.

Have the imagination necessary to turn the most menial of tasks into adventures.
Make your life have the sort of occurrences that you would like to experience,
And do not become so staid in your routine that it becomes a burden.
Please yourself with the simple pleasures that grant satisfaction in all you do.

July 13th, 1993
(Part B)

When the most perfect person comes into your life,
It is always best to be ready to accept what is offered.
Do not let pride or foolishness keep you apart.
Be happy that you have found each other.

The miracle of having someone to share your life with does not come often;
So, you are completely foolish if you do anything to block it.
Be what it is you are, and let the event of your meeting take place in it's own time.
You cannot rush things of this nature, but you must also not let them slip away.

July 13th, 1993
(Part C)

The completeness of a human depends entirely upon the mate.
When there is none, no person can possibly be whole.
There must be that joining of two souls to one that makes for unity,
And if you feel you are whole alone, you are just fooling yourself.

July 13th, 1993
(Part D)

Going about the business of life,
Whether it is simple or complex,
All depends upon one's point of view.
So, live while you may, and think of nothing but how to make things better.

The world is so full of pessimistic people,
And most seem to be out only for themselves,
That anyone found that only wants to help,
Should be encouraged in that endeavor, and should themselves be helped to promote that end.

July 15th, 1993

Realizing all of the dreams that you have had are attainable,
And being able to bring them to completion,
Will give one a sense of satisfaction that is hard to compare with anything else.
If you don't realize your dreams, simply dream of something else, and try for that.

The reality of the world is such that everyone must work for their existence,
And those who do not, will not last very long in the competition.
Be as content as you can with what you are doing,
Because there may not be anything else that you can do with what you have.

Understanding your limitations and being able to work through them,
Gives one a sense of pride in the fact that you have the ability to reason through difficulties.
Be not worried about the imposed limits of society;
Only concern yourself with those you impose upon yourself.

July 15th, 1993
(Part B)

Being right does not constitute license;
And being wrong does not mean incompetence;
Both are interchangeable with changing criteria.
So, do not believe that once right you will never be wrong again.

July 16th, 1993

When the pressures of living in this all to hard world,
Becomes so great that you feel you must have some release;
Give thanks that we live when we do;
For in other times you might not be able to withstand the world as it was or is.

Become whatever it is that you feel will make you happy,
And don't think of choosing between one form of drudgery and another.
Focus on all of the good things that fill your life.
You will be more pleased and content that way than any other.

Do not let boredom overcome what was once an exciting experience.
Make it exciting once more by infusing new life into your world.
Overcome that feeling of sameness which prevails over the soul at times,
And prosper at the aspect of something new happening each day.

July 16th, 1993
(Part B)

Involve yourself with people of all types,
And do not stop simply because there are some bad experiences.
Continue to put it on the line for those that appreciate it.
There are many instances where the things and people you touch will prove meaningful.

July 19th, 1993

Beginning to understand the needs and emotions of your mate,
Without the necessity for prolonged inquiry into the matter,
Is the start of what is known as living for the other, and love.
This state of affairs happens to those truly in love, and it doesn't matter how short or long a time they have been together.

When the needs of your mate outweigh your own in your mind,
You have attained that plateau of love which comes but rarely.
You should count yourself among the extremely lucky if your mate feels the same.
Do not let outside influence or happenstance come between you.

Awaken each day with a sense of wonder at the possibilities of a new day.
Especially one in which you will be joined with your lover.
Be optimistic at the opportunities which present themselves in whatever guise,
And take advantage of each moment spent in working toward your joint goal.

July 19th, 1993
(Part B)

Perhaps being a dreamer is not the best pragmatic way to live in this world;
But better to dream of possibilities of Utopia on earth than to be caught with only selfish desires.
The only people that will be remembered by history,
Are those that dared to dream of something better for the whole, rather than just their own small piece of humanity.

July 19th, 1993
(Part C)

Coming to the realization that you cannot make right every wrong,
And you have little control over the injustices perpetrated by society,
Might tend to give some people the perspective that they should no longer try.
Do not be among those, attempt to change what you can and at least participate.

Withdrawing from the pursuit of justice for your fellow man,
Does not exclude you from having injustices perpetrated against you;
It only makes it easier to have them visited upon everyone.
Use your voice in whatever means available to help those in need, and you will never be left with regrets.

July 21st, 1993

Discovering what you are best suited for in this life,
And finding that it interests you and quite possibly will make you happy,
Is perhaps the biggest achievement any of us aspire to.
So, do not despair if you haven't found it, yet, just keep looking.

July 22nd, 1993

The everlasting truth that no one is meant to live alone,
May seem not so evident to some whom think they do just fine on their own.
But without other people, you really are not living a whole existence;
And without someone special to share with, you do not know what you have missed.

Being sentient implies that you can interact with others;
So, do not fall into the trap of only allowing certain people close.
Take a chance on as many others as seem prudent,
And trust your intuition about people to steer you clear of those that would harm you.

July 23rd, 1993

When contemplating the state of your life,
Keep in mind that many others have done the same;
And of all those, none have come up with a universal answer for all.
Everyone must find their own solutions, but it is always helpful to listen to others.

Just because the universal answer has eluded us up until now,
Does not mean that we should no longer search for it.
It only means that none as yet has found it;
But I believe that answer lies with sharing your life with someone special.

If there are no other constants in the world besides the love you share,
That should be all that you need to withstand the outside world.
No one should be able to intercede upon your bastion of love,
Not anyone at all.

July 23rd, 1993
(Part B)

To work all your life towards a goal that is worthwhile,
And to have attained that goal at a point in time that is not at the end of your life,
May sometimes bring a slight let down to your spirits;
But you should let that be as it may, and go on to set new goals.

The best way to overcome some small depression is to force yourself to be active.
Not letting any other thoughts come into your mind except those that lead to some action.
Simply giving in to depression is the surest way to make it last,
And sometimes a little depression is good, but never over do it.

The happiest people in the world are those that have found someone special;
And they thank their maker for the opportunities they have each day to do for the other.
When you have no one whom you care for more than yourself,
You have not fulfilled yourself, and you are cheating someone out of being fulfilled.

July 26th, 1993

Wondering from where the most suited mate for you is coming,
And not really knowing if you will ever be so blessed,
Might cause anxiety in the most calm of us.
If you are patient, the opportunity will present itself, and happiness can be obtained.

Traveling through this life in expectation of fulfilling your dreams,
Begins with a first step to make those dreams reality.
There are many that never even venture to make the first move,
So, consider that when you have any kind of little set back.

What makes the difference between a winner and an also ran,
Is entirely the attitude brought to the competition.
There are many opportunities for all of us,
If we would but open ourselves to them.

July 27th, 1993

Longing for cessation to the mundane struggle for existence,
And wondering how others cope with these same problems,
Brings a sense of unity among all.
There may never be a respite to drudgery, but be thankful for the good times that break up the spans.

July 28th, 1993

Appreciate the people closest to you.
Attempt not to take for granted all that is done by them for you.
Because there are so few people that you will meet that will accept you for what you are;
And just because you have friends, do not think that they will forever remain so, if abused.

The quality of your acquaintances will only improve if you do;
So, you must endeavor to become whatever it is that you can feel good about.
Life is so short, all time wasted on selfish endeavors should be cut to a minimum,
And the time spent thinking of and doing for others should be expanded.

July 30th, 1993

The very presence or absence of some people can make you happy or sad.
For some it is their absence that bring joy, and with others, their presence.
If you find that the people that make you happy by their absence number more than the others,
Then perhaps it is you that should examine your feelings and attitudes towards others.

Be consoled with the prospect of finding good people in the world,
And feel not impatient if they do not come all at once to your door.
When something is worthwhile, it usually takes some time;
And a little effort on your part to be pleasant would not hurt.

August 2nd, 1993

We experience the wonder of love with only a select few in this world;
And those that share this with us are to be reassured.
There may be other joys and good things in this world,
But someone to love is by far the greatest of these, and makes everything else so much better.

Bring the ultimate experience back into your life,
And make every day a day to be remembered.
If you have the capacity to truly love someone,
Then you should not withhold that love for any reason.

August 3rd, 1993

Being peculiar to some people is a badge that is worn proudly;
While others shun their company for this peculiarity they possess.
We are all somewhat peculiar in that we all are different,
And we should accept these differences with aplomb.

Being the kind of world that it is,
We do not have much control over the people we must work with;
But we will be remembered for those we choose to be our friends,
So, select carefully, and invest some time in those friends.

August 4th, 1993

Attaining a maturity suitable for the proper interaction with others,
Takes time and help from those closest to you.
There may be some short cuts to reaching maturity,
But most leave out the very necessary aspect of time.

The mental and emotional growth attained with time,
Cannot be gained in some crash course given by a third party.
The only valid method of maturing is going through all of life's experiences yourself.
No one else can do this for you.

The process can be helped along with the finding of a good mate.
If you can borrow some understanding from that mate, so much the better.
Do not become totally dependent upon the best thing in your life;
For then you will loose part of yourself in the other.

August 4th, 1993
(Part B)

The balance needed in life is best found in the eyes of another.
There could well be well rounded individuals that are alone,
But the number is not large.
For the needs of anyone cannot be met alone.

August 5th, 1993

Many in this world are blessed with the love of a spouse,
And they have the honor of returning that love in kind.
For those without such luck, there is still hope,
And when they have found someone, they will understand what was missing.

The coming of age brings with it responsibility for others and yourself;
And when you understand that all must live with and for others,
You will appreciate life more, and those that have helped you.
Give of yourself to all that ask, and help those you can.

August 5th, 1993
(Part B)

When confronted with a problem which is beyond your understanding,
And there seems to be no other help in sight,
You may do well to dissect the problem and attack each part,
Rather than to simply give up before you start.

Become amenable to help when offered,
Do not obstinately keep trying old answers to new situations,
Because those old methods may have worked once does not mean they will always prove useful.
By all means be adaptable.

August 6th, 1993
To Rhonda Pomeroy

When all the problems, dependencies, or addictions have been labeled,
And you feel that you are justified in continuing your behavior because of this,
You have reached the point where any justification will do, so long as you can continue with your immature behavior.
This may get you through a day or two, but it will not last a life time.

You can stroke your conscience all you like with explanations,
And some of the help you can obtain may be actually useful;
But in the end you must take responsibility fro your own actions,
And live like a mature adult without looking for other sources or people to blame for your problems.

August 6th, 1993
(Part B)

Collect all the good will that others allow you,
And return that sentiment to all you may justify to deserve it;
Because there are no hermits any longer that are successful,
You should bring yourself to life with new incentive to commingle.

August 9th, 1993

Aspiring to excellence in all you undertake,
And not being satisfied with what you consider to be less,
Will keep you ever endeavoring to be better than you were.
But if you judge yourself to harshly, you might fall victim to depression.

Strive for the best you can do,
And reward yourself for every minor accomplishment.
Just because you have not done something perfectly,
Do not overlook the fact that you have truly attempted to do the best you could.

August 10th, 1993

It may seem that the help needed by some is indeterminable,
And that no matter how much you give, they still demand more.
It often leads to speculation on whether they have any sense of responsibility at all,
And perhaps they do not, but there is the chance that they may develop it with time and the right help.

August 11th, 1993

The morning of each new day brings with it an opportunity for improvement;
There may not be very much change, but any could be for the better.
Be consoled that many may find dread in the new day,
But if you are of these, attempt to change your perspective.

August 13th, 1993

Lamenting on poor luck and bemoaning what fate has done to you,
Does nothing to enhance your plight.
All which must be done to improve your lot is the opposite of what went before.
You must make an effort to recognize that yours are not insoluble problems if you will address them with thought.

Be a little more concerned with others and their problems,
For if you can help with theirs', you should be more able to gain a new approach to your own.
Do not think that shutting yourself away from others will help,
It only makes for more self pity and deeper depression.

August 13th, 1993
(Part B)

Concluding that life is worth living after all,
Is the beginning of recovery from depression and most other mental ailments.
Leaving all of the things you can do nothing about for others,
Is the first step toward solving the problems that you can.

Have patience with those you deal with that haven't yet seen that light,
And you will last longer than otherwise possible.
Because there may or may not be something you can do to change people,
You should know that the only person you have control over is yourself.

Give time to the betterment of your own attitude,
And you will influence those around you.
If you only tell others what to do,
You will have almost no lasting impact on them or anyone else.

August 17th, 1993

Coming to terms with the opposing forces within,
Is a major step in fulfilling yourself as a whole person.
Although the path is strewn with pitfalls,
The goal is worth every bit of effort expended in the attaining.

The most wondrous thing that we all can do,
Is to fulfill our personal goals and share ourselves with others.
Although there may be some that do not wish to be so blessed,
Most likely that is because they themselves are not fulfilled.

August 18th, 1993

There can be beauty found in all that you encounter,
The trick is to adjust your eye and mind to look for it.
All that is necessary for a truly meaningful outlook,
Is the correct frame of mind that doesn't prejudge on appearances.

There might be any number of reasons to find fault in something or someone,
But if you wish to improve your own view of life,
You should look in earnest for those things that may be admired.
Always finding fault does nothing but bring negative feelings to you and those around you.

Leave all nonconstructive criticism out of your relationships,
And you will find that you will have more worthwhile ones.
The people attracted to positive attitudes are more numerous than the opposite,
And they will be more likely to be themselves and open with you.

August 18th, 1993
(Part B)

Understanding what you can of others motives and actions,
There are some that will defy all logic.
For those you must simply bypass or take a direct approach and simply ask point blank.
But do not be caught by pretenses that really have no basis or motivation.

August 18th, 1993
(Part C)

In quest for the meaning behind every action,
Whether or not there is meaning for all actions.
The search for enlightenment will take us through a lifetime;
And the answers we find will give a sense of accomplishment, however
fleeting.

The obsession with cause and effect as a method of solving all problems,
Will not necessarily obtain for you the answers you desire in all cases.
Be prepared to take some things on faith,
And you will have a less troubled path through this life.

August 19th, 1993

Wondering from wince the next inspiration will come,
With thoughts as to where there could have been good ideas,
Will force a kind of yearning for something better than what we have.
No amount of prosperity and success seems to quench this thirst for improvement.

August 19th, 1993
(Part B)

Wishing to become the best that you can be,
Is a phase that we all go through at one time or another.
And it helps to realize that if we have expended our best effort,
Then we have actually won the struggle.

August 19th, 1993
(Part C)

When going out late into the world to conquer your goals and dreams,
Think only of how this may be accomplished without harm to others.
For this is the only method of succeeding that will satisfy all concerned;
And you will be helped along the way by those you associate with.

August 19th, 1993
(Part D)

When you number your friends and you cannot seem to count them all,
You are a very lucky person.
But if you are like most of us,
Your true friends are very few.

Most probably there are good reasons for only having a few good friends,
And the only worthwhile friends you have,
Are those that ask not what you can do for them,
But how they may help you.

August 23rd, 1993

Removing obstacles from your path to happiness and well being,
Is a full time occupation for all so inclined to believe that these are reachable goals.
And for those that do not think there is hope for them,
They must be brought to see that it is possible for everyone.

Only when you loose hope is there the greatest obstacle in your path;
For without hope little seems achievable in life.
You loose something of yourself in a pessimistic attitude toward life.
Where there is hope, there is always a way to inner and outer peace.

August 23rd, 1993
(Part B)

The beauty of having someone that loves you and your love in return,
Is a miracle to be nourished by both people concerned.
There may be times when it seems that not much is happening between
you,
But those are just the comfortable times of togetherness.

Appreciate the happy times you have shared with one another,
And try not to take each other for granted.
It is when you do this that there may be the chance of separateness.
Be on your guard against the seeds of thoughtlessness.

August 26th, 1993

Coming to the conclusion that no one has all the answers you need,
And realizing that at best the solutions to life's major problems are not at all easy to find,
Will bring a tolerance for others' problems and their attempts at solution.
Be advised that what you put into solutions, will be returned to you just that much.

August 31st, 1993

As the years go by and you find yourself feeling their effect,
Be thankful for whatever measure of fitness that you possess.
There are many that do not have as much as you.
Be as steadfast in your resolve as ever and have no doubts as to your course.

September 2nd, 1993

Understand that we are not alone with our problems,
That there is help for even the most incorrigible of us.
And no matter how dismal the outlook may appear at present,
There is always the hope of a brighter tomorrow.

Place your trust in your fellow man, and whatever God you believe in,
And there is always the chance that through it all, you will overcome.
Do not let pride and doubt rule your life,
For these have their place, but not as the governing factor in a healthy existence.

September 2nd 1993
(Part B)

When suitable partners come together to share life's pursuits between them,
It can be the most rewarding experience for both;
Or it can be made unpleasant by either person.
The difference is what both people bring with them, and what both are willing to compromise on.

Leaving the security of home to venture out for whatever reason,
May often seem the only recourse to retain what home life you have.
The greatest risk is not having the will to put yourself through whatever it takes to keep your home together.
Often people fall victim to depression of soul that counts nothing as valuable.

September 3rd, 1993

Bless the eternal optimist for his seeming unreasoning cheerfulness.
The bright outlook granted to these individuals does stem from logic;
They simply slant their view toward finding something good from all situations and people.
The other side of the coin is not so bright, and these people will find doom and gloom in almost everything.

September 7th, 1993

When confronted with the prospect of continued pain,
Whether it is mental, emotional or physical, we all would rather find a method to dispel it;
Sometimes there is no easy way to procure relief,
But it is better to make the effort, than to live with agony.

We all must face the core fact that in most cases concerning mental and emotional pain,
We are the ones that bring it upon ourselves.
When you get to the bottom line, only we can ease this stress for ourselves.
There may or may not be simple answers to discomfort cessation, but we should not discount anything that works.

Put your trust in yourself to be able to handle anything that comes your way,
For without this trust, you will never be wholly adequate at any task.
There are many that go through life looking outside themselves for answers,
And sometimes this can work, but for any basic needs, you must rely upon yourself.

September 7th, 1993
(Part B)

The happiness which comes from two lives joined,
Is hard to match with any other type of joy.
The sharing and caring for each other does not diminish with time when the union is right,
And the correct type of union is hard to find, so do not let it slip by.

Create your happiness by living for someone else,
And you will find many rewards in store for both of you.
There are as many types of joy as there are couples in the world;
And when you find your match, you too will begin to experience them.

September 8th, 1993

Bring your whole attention to what you are spending your time on,
And try not to be distracted by things beyond your control;
For the simple reason that anything worth doing is worth doing well.
Do not let being a perfectionist get in the way of completing a project.

September 9th, 1993

To become all that you wish to be is perhaps the most difficult and frustrating problem in life;
For there are so many things that you would like to do,
And so little actual time in which to accomplish them all.
The best course is to work more on the things that have the most meaning for you, and let the others wait.

All of us wish for something better in our lives than what we seem to have,
And that is good, because we can look forward to that better day.
Just because we have not accomplished what we would most desire,
Does not mean that we will not.

September 19th, 1993

Coping with the everyday annoyances that we all must face,
Entails that we keep our heads and not make any rash actions.
There are many ways in which we can make it through each day,
But not becoming overwrought by life's obstacles will give you the best chance of success.

September 13th, 1993

There may be times when there seems to be no alternative to boredom,
And to combat complacency you look for anything at all with the aspect of newness.
Look inward for a new approach to this age old problem,
And perhaps you would find more to take the place of the hum drum than you imagined possible.

Finding fault with all that comes your way in life,
Is not a healthy method for dealing with life's problems.
There are many good things that may be found in everyone and everything.
The biggest obstacle in many peoples' paths is their perspective.

September 13th, 1993
(Part B)

Wondering where the time goes that you are apart from your mate,
And wishing for more time together without fear of having to much;
Brings us all into the reality that is life,
And to the conclusion that there should be a better way to live.

There could be more than ordinary work to supply us with what we need to exist,
And for those who have found the method,
They wonder how they ever got along without it.
For those of us still in the struggle, we must cope the best we can.

The greatest of all possible worlds would be one in which we all enjoy what we do,
And there would be no regrets to time lost in endeavors that we really did not enjoy.
Everyone should look to the times when they are fulfilling themselves,
As the ones to be remembered and cherished.

September 17th, 1993

With each passing day the opportunities we mess accumulate,
And for the ones that cannot be put off to another day, They are perhaps forever gone.
We do take advantage of some of those chances,
And for those we should appreciate that we have recognized them.

There are many people that will overlook all opportunities of every day,
And for those lucky enough or perceptive enough not to,
They will have made better use of each day than the others.
Do not bemoan yesterday's loses, look to today and all the days ahead.

September 17th, 1993
(Part B)

Strive to comprehend all you can about the reasoning behind others' actions,
For with understanding comes acceptance and a better opportunity for self appreciation.
Those of us who look at the world with blinders on,
Will have little chance to broaden their horizons beyond their own perspective.

Being willing to accept others for what they are and have to offer,
Gives us all hope to better understand and like ourselves.
Those people that bring an open mind to life,
Have a much easier time adapting to all of life's' occurrences.

September 22nd, 1993

Feeling good about life is a perspective that we all should strive for,
And there are many reasons why we should feel good.
If you should be of the number that does not,
Take a closer look at all you have to feel good about.

Being in a position that does not allow for any regrets is enviable,
And very few of us ever reach this point.
The less time spent in pondering what might have been,
The more time may be spent in doing something about matters at hand.

September 22nd, 1993
(Part B)

To understand the people around you, you must first understand yourself.
There may be all the best intentions in the world on your part to help,
But misplaced comprehension of the problem negates any help offered.
Take the first step on the path, and search your inner self for enlightenment.

Many of us are in need of help of one type or another,
And any that boast they need no such assistance are only making it harder on themselves.
There are those which see asking for help to be a sign of inadequacy,
But there should be no such feeling, because we all need each other at some time.

September 22nd, 1993
(Part C)

The wonder that is having a partner to share life's' triumphs and trials,
Is a miracle that happens infrequently in everyone's life.
If you should find another that you may share your inner most self with,
Then you have reached the goal of the life long search for fulfillment.

When things become a little tedious,
And there seems to be no end to the struggle of getting through the day,
You should think of your mate, and all the wonderful things she does for you.
There might be times when you are not at your best, but she can turn that around.

Often in life you might daydream about things you would like to do,
And if you have someone to daydream with and about,
You will find that some of those dreams will come to pass.
The only way to true happiness in life is found when you live for another.

September 22nd, 1993
(Part D)

Understanding comes with time,
And all you do with the time you have has some meaning,
Whether it is apparent at present or not is dependent upon your viewpoint;
So do not feel that any time you spend is wasted, look for some redeeming aspect.

When you have all you have wished for at your call,
And there seems no other thing that you would want,
Then if you also have someone to share these things with,
You have truly fulfilled not only yourself, but that other person as well.

Be comfortable with yourself and others around you,
For not to be causes not only you stress, but the others, also.
Do not worry about how you might affect others,
For all that begets is more tension for yourself.

September 22nd, 1993
(Part E)

Golden gems of wisdom are not so hard to come by,
If you look at the everyday occurrences of life and apply common sense.
You will have taken a large step in procuring some for yourself.
Some of the most significant thought is accomplished by using horse sense.

September 22nd, 1993
(Part F)

The consolation prize in life is often worth more than the grand prize,
If you know how to appreciate the finer things of living.
Then any and everything should be a great benefit to you.
There are many with so little that even a dollar would make a difference.

September 23rd, 1993

Become the type of person which cares about the plight of others,
And be not concerned how this might seem to your peers;
Because everyone in this world must be free of constant need,
In order for all to be truly free.

September 24th, 1993

There are so many things to be thankful for in this life,
But sometimes we forget how luck we are to be able to live how we choose.
In many parts of the world there is no such freedom,
And for all those not so blessed, it is an accomplishment to have even a small measure of happiness.

September 24th, 1993
(Part B)

Enjoy the people and things about you while you may,
For our time on this earth is measured and no one knows when his will be up.
Everyone and everything has something to offer to our interest,
And only the close minded will find nothing offered by all.

During the course of our lives we often overlook the everyday enjoyments that we might make use of,
And all the more to our despair, we miss some really nice aspects of people and things around us.
There may be reasons why we have become hardened to the little niceties of life,
But we should endeavor to ponder and appreciate them whenever we can remember to do so.

September 24th, 1993
(Part C)

Consider yourself an integral part of the life we all share on this world,
And treat yourself with care and understanding so that you may do the same for others.
Do not fall into the trap of self incrimination and depreciation,
Give yourself credit where due, and attempt to improve in all other areas.

September 27th, 1993

The bitterness which some bring to life each day has no logical foundation,
It has simply become a way of life for them and this is sad.
There is no worse method of living than to be so negative about everything,
And for all those that choose to live in this manner, there should be an enlightenment of hope.

September 27th, 1993

The bitterness which some bring to life each day has no logical foundation,
It has simply become a way of life for them, and this is sad.
There is no worse method of living than to be so negative about everything,
And for all those that choose to live in this manner, there should be an enlightenment of hope.

September 27th, 1993
(Part B)

Coming to the dance of life with no preconceptions about what steps to take is sometimes good;
Although you probably will not dazzle anyone with your foot work, you will be open to new concepts.
There are many professed experts that really do not know what to do when confronted with something different,
And all those with little experience treat everything as different.

September 27th, 1993
(Part C)

Console yourself with all the good things accomplished when
something goes awry,
For not all you undertake will have a beneficial result to all concerned.
Look not for ways to correct things long past,
Instead attempt to learn by past mistakes and not to repeat them
endlessly.

All that hear the cross of being human will make mistakes in life,
And to be unforgiving is to be hypocritical;
Because few of us could live long if we did not forgive ourselves,
And everyone else should be afforded the same consideration.

September 27th, 1993
(Part D)

For all these people that would wish for an easier life,
And all those whom think they have found one,
All our luck on achieving this goal, for not many will ever attain it.
Do not become disheartened at what you must do to survive as you wish to.

Becoming a happy person is sometimes the hardest thing in the world to do.
You must overcome all of your inner obstacles which block your path,
And then you must learn to make lemonade out of all the lemons life has a tendency of handing you.
So, do not become frustrated, and keep on trying to find your share of happiness.

September 28th, 1993

The wonder of being alive should not be taken for granted,
And if you are in good health, that is another blessing that is sometimes overlooked.
So appreciate what you have, and try to share the good feeling with those around you,
And you will see the difference in your own life as well as others.

When you take things for granted that really should not be,
And you become somewhat insensitive to others,
You have let yourself become prone to discontent.
This is not good for you or the people you associate with.

September 28th, 1993
(Part B)

When it seems that most things are going poorly on a given day,
And perhaps you are tired of trying to make it come out right,
Think of the pleasure derived from your abilities at most times,
And not of the unsuccessful tasks of today, for there will be tomorrow.

September 29th, 1993

There are many ways to fulfill yourself and help others,
And there are no wrong methods, except where others are injured.
So, do not attempt to exactly emulate any one method to self illumination;
Take the best of any method you fancy and piece together your own.

Being entirely human, we all must face the facts that we will make mistakes,
And we should not be to hard on ourselves for this short coming.
Instead, we should try not to make the same miscue again and again,
And give our hard fought wisdom the chance to help someone else avoid a pitfall.

September 29th, 1993
(Part B)

Collecting all the trivial facts that are needed to fill the corners of our minds,
Is a full time occupation for some, and just comes naturally for others.
There seems no end to the number of things and ideas we clutter our minds with,
And if we are lucky we will retain all this data for our entire lives.

Although some feel that to unnecessarily retain a lot of facts is not beneficial,
And we should make more effort to retain the knowledge of how to get the facts,
It is still pleasurable to be able to call upon some obscure fact when needed.
Confidentially, I feel the move valuable is the knowledge of "how to" rather than the simple facts themselves.

September 30th, 1993

Stepping from one aspect of reality to another,
Entails something as simple as conversing with one then another person,
Or it could be a complete mind shift from one point of view to another.
We all experience these changes, for life is made up of them.

When we have mastered the subtleties of these shifts,
Without undue personality shifts and stress,
Then we have attained a maturity of mind that we all must achieve.
Give thought to how you may better retain this maturity and carry forth your relationships with others in this light.

"Building a Relationship"
September 30th, 1993

Begin with the things you both share in common,
Build new interests together as the opportunities arise,
And maintain the sense of freshness that a new relationship brings.
This should work for any couple just starting, and for those together for a time.

Understand that you will each have your previous experience to call upon,
And most times this will help in avoiding some of the miscues.
But when all else fails, you should spend time talking about your problems,
And whenever needed, compromise.

To build a lasting relationship first takes liking each other,
Then love must be the building block upon which to form your match.
There should always be honesty between you,
And a sensitivity for each others' feelings and needs.

Look not to others to help you through the tough times,
But to each other for support and understanding.
When you can no longer bear the thought of being apart,
You have come to the pinnacle of the most beautiful bond between two people.

October 4th, 1993

The beauty which surrounds us is sometimes overlooked,
And even the best of us are prone to take the everyday for granted.
But with each day we should take a few minutes to appreciate some ordinary aspect of life,
For it is a miracle that each day we get the opportunity to experience these ordinary things.

Hold the truly beautiful with respect and awe that such deserves,
And you will begin to appreciate everything much more.
Do not be filled with jealousy for those that seem to have it all,
For everyone has their cross to bear, and the jealous only really hurt themselves.

October 7th, 1993

When confronted with a problem that seems insurmountable,
And fresh answers are needed in place of the old,
Look to your feelings and intuition for the best possible result.
Over analyzing may not be quite so productive as a method of solution finding.

There are no problems which do not have some solution,
And if you work at any one of them long enough, the answer will come.
Do not be frustrated if no quick solution can be found,
There is almost always enough time to dig out the best answer.

October 7th, 1993
(Part B)

Realizing that you are human and prone to mistakes may disappoint some,
But those that have accepted the human condition are much less prone to stress and discontent with themselves.
So, be of good cheer while traversing life's' path,
And forgive yourself your mistakes and try not to make the same ones again.

October 7th, 1993
(Part C)

Perchance to find a truly good person on this world,
Is, perhaps, one of the nicest things that can happen;
And to take advantage of good people when you find them,
Is one of the worse things that we can do.

Some people seem hell bent on using others to their own ends,
And of these there are few that can truly sleep with a clear conscience.
Do not wonder why you are taken advantage of,
Just be thankful that you are not being unfair to others.

October 8th, 1993

Beginning to understand your purpose in life is an awakening.
It will change your outlook on almost everything that you are involved with,
And you will no longer have so many anxious moments of feeling you should be doing something else.
All of us are in the same boat when it comes to finally discovering our meaning.

For those of us lucky enough to have gotten this enlightenment early in life,
There is still the prospect of new adventure with other people,
And for those of us that seem to come by it late, there is the satisfaction of working long and hard toward the reachable goal.
Everyone has an over powering urge to have their life possess a meaning beyond the simple necessities of living.

October 8th, 1993
(Part B)

To live a faultless life is not to be human,
For we all have made some mistakes in the process of living.
But to be as error free as possible almost qualities as faultless;
So, do not be to hard on yourself for making what seems to you to be a lot of mistakes.

Forgiving yourself for your miscues is a start at relieving stress,
And if you can forgive yourself you should certainly be able to forgive others.
Do not fall into the snare of thinking that all you do is correct,
Because no one is without flaw.

October 8th, 1993
(Part C)

Leave all preconceptions about people behind when meeting anew,
For you do injustice to the people you meet if you try to categorize them.
This is not to say that you should forget all past experience,
Just give each person you meet a fair chance to stand or fall on his or her own merits.

October 11th, 1993

The cold overcast mornings of Fall seem to put a damper on our souls,
And there may be no help except the passing of Fall and Winter into Spring.
But there are those people that carry Spring with them no matter the season,
And for those we should all be thankful.

October 11th, 1993
(Part B)

To carry with you a feeling of newness and excitement,
Takes a very optimistic and sometimes naive frame of mind.
All of the things you do each day may seem to be the same old routine,
But if you can ingest freshness into all, you will have a much better chance of maintaining a good attitude.

October 13th, 1993

The morning of each new day can be an exciting new opportunity or something you just try to get through,
It all depends upon your perspective and how you look at life.
For those just attempting to make it through, there is not much chance of pleasure in the things they do,
But for the others every task is another step in the building of enjoyment of the day.

October 13th, 1993
(Part B)

While there are those of us that feel everything we undertake has meaning,
And that there is an underlying purpose to all that everyone does,
There are also those that feel they are simply treading water.
For these there is not much brilliance in the sparkle of each new day.

Look for any meaning that you can possibly see in all that you do,
And try to help others see that all tasks undertaken are of some importance.
Just because you cannot see the benefit immediately,
Do not label a chore as without substance.

October 14th, 1993

The budding of a new relationship is a fragile thing that must be nourished,
And it takes both parties exercising care and tenderness to each other to flourish.
When one is simply out to use the other, there can be no true bond between them,
And often both parties suffer from the resulting discord this causes.

Go gently on your path to a lasting relationship,
And try not to force one with the first person you encounter.
For the right one is out there somewhere if you will take the time to look,
And there is no substitute for the match you were meant for.

When it seems that finding someone to share your dreams with is beyond your grasp,
Remember that everyone has been there during their lives,
And so long as you do not withdraw from the search,
You will eventually succeed and keep hope alive for others as well.

October 15th, 1993

When you have found the key to your happiness,
And the world has beaten a path to your door for the secret,
The temptation is to share your secret,
But you may find it only works for you.

October 15th, 1993
(Part B)

Following the lead of all profound lovers,
We might just stumble upon a combination that works.
And when you may truly classify yourself in that group,
Then others will try to emulate what you have accomplished.

When you place your lovers' needs above your own,
And whatever makes her happy is what also brings joy to you,
Then you have found what can only be called true love.
You should cherish this match for all of time.

October 15th, 1993
(Part C)

Wonder about the miracles that occur everyday,
For each morning when the sun comes up is a miracle,
And every blade of grass and tree and flower are also miracles of life.
So, try to be amazed by all the wonders around you, not on what does not seem to go your way.

October 18th, 1993

Leaving doubts behind you is an important step in beginning to trust yourself,
And there are many instances in which a little self questioning can be helpful.
For a healthy attitude toward yourself, you should not question everything you do,
And for a start you should trust yourself not to make simple mistakes into large ones.

October 18th, 1993
(Part B)

Comprehension of your problems is the only way you can hope to overcome them,
And it is no easy task to understand every aspect of your own problems.
It seems much easier to grasp the problems of someone else rather than our own,
And not everyone can distance themselves to undertake an objective analysis of themselves.

All the self help theories in the world will not help anyone who does not understand themselves,
And for those that fully understand, the self help theories are not applicable.
So, for those of us wishing to better ourselves,
We need to start with the basic concept of understanding ourselves.

October 19th, 1993

On a dark and gloomy Autumn day it is easy to give in to depression,
The sign of those who will not succumb is the cheerful attitude they possess even on these days.
It may seem no easy matter to maintain a good outlook on life,
But it will become simpler as you gain in practice.

Be pleasant to those around you when you are tempted not to be,
And you will have surpassed many that cannot be happy with anything.
There are many reasons you can find to be unhelpful and unpleasant,
But you will find that being the opposite is much easier to maintain.

October 19th, 1993
(Part B)

Leaving aside the perceived differences between you and others,
Takes a special aspect of being that is mature enough to realize that seeming differences really matter little,
And that there are more important things to focus on with others.
Do not fall victim to obstinacy of perspective, leave yourself open to new thought.

October 20th, 1993

To be a part of the human experience is to have regrets of things done in the past,
And to have found remembrances of other aspects of your life.
It is to strive for better actions on your part that will help others,
And it is sometimes to be selfish when your better self would not want you to be.

There are as many types of people as you could possibly imagine,
And for this diversity we should be thankful.
For what a dull world it would be with only one or two kinds,
And there would not be the opportunities of changing yourself in any degree.

Even the best of us sometimes wonder why there cannot be more for themselves,
And to fall prey to the wishing for a better circumstance is often counter productive.
Best to be thankful for our gifts and abilities and those we call friend,
Than to wish for more and not work at trying to obtain it.

October 20th, 1993
(Part B)

Taking into consideration all the woes of mankind is counter productive;
It leaves you with a sense of despair that is sometimes hard to overcome.
Let the good balance the bad, for that is how life is,
And you will find plenty to appreciate if you look enough.

October 20th, 1993
(Part C)

When the Fall leafs begin to turn,
And the color is everywhere to see,
We are reminded of the wonderful cycle that we enjoy,
And of all the prospects ahead of us to experience.

Looking for all the world as if there might be no tomorrow,
Some gray and dismal days just seem to beg us to stay in bed.
Being able to overcome that sloth is one of the things that separates us from animals,
And the ability to find some redeeming quality in the day is another.

October 22nd, 1993

Caring for someone is not all there is to love;
There is also sharing all your dreams, idiosyncrasies, and triumphs and failures.
In addition you should put the happiness of others before your own,
And they should do like wise for you.

Most couples together in the world do not really appreciate all they do for each other,
And for those that do, all the hardships that might befall them will be as water off a duck's back.
There is not storm that true love cannot weather,
And it takes very little for other types of relationships to falter.

The greatest success that anyone can achieve in life,
Means little without a partner to share it with.
The truly lucky ones find their mate,
And consider themselves the most successful people in the world.

October 26th, 1993

Bringing yourself to understand what it is that you are about,
Without the recriminations of feeling you might have done some things differently,
Is the key to becoming self confident and assured in your actions.
This maturing may take a life time, or you may find it early in life, be patient.

Some people travel blissfully through life with no thought of self analysis,
And for some this may be a perfectly good way to pursue life's goals.
For most of us there are always those times when we question our actions,
And the methods we employ to solve life's problems.

Giving thought to how we pursue our dreams,
And how best to make them reality,
Is one of life's most interesting puzzles.
The one we spend most of our time trying to solve.

October 26th, 1993
(Part B)

Leaving behind all thought of self indulgence,
And taking up the banner of the good Samaritan,
Is what we should all do on occasion.
But realistically we do not do so quite often enough.

October 26th, 1993
(Part C)

Become as independent as you possibly may,
Keeping in mind that no one can stand completely alone.
For the less you depend upon others the greater your chances of not being let down.
So, have not the expectation of someone solving all your problems and you will learn to solve them yourself.

October 26th, 1993
(Part D)

Live as though there were to be no tomorrow,
And you might be caught short when it arrives.
Temper your indulgences with thought for the future,
For there will be a tomorrow for the great majority of us.

October 26th, 1993
(Part E)

When able, lead the way to a better place,
When not, follow gracefully the path offered by another.
If there be no path offered, bide your time,
For the opportunity for improvement will come, you simply must choose when to participate.

November 4th, 1993

Consider the blessing bestowed upon you by all of life's pleasures;
The most note worthy of which is your continued existence on this wonderful world.
If you should have someone to share this life with,
Then you are by far one of the truly lucky ones.

When you finally discern for yourself that you can only go so far blaming someone else,
And you understand that you must undertake to make your life better,
You have achieved over half the battle toward maturity.
There is no one that will take responsibility for all of your obligations and needs, except yourself.

These may be hard realities to face,
But unless you do, you will never be the kind of person you might otherwise become.
There are no easy methods of finding yourself, once lost,
And you must find it within yourself to turn the tables on temptations.

Whether or not you make it in this world is almost entirely up to you.
You may get help along the way,
But it is you that must depend solely upon yourself for your peace of mind.
There could well be no easy path, but you make it impossible by blaming someone else.

October 27th, 1993

Balling back on the aspects of living that come easiest to you,
Will probably get you through most of life.
There are some things that you will have to invent new methods for,
And these are the key to whether or not you can succeed in any situation.

October 28th, 1993

Accepting your faults and working around them to accomplish your goals,
When it seems that no amount of hard work will help.
Persevering and succeeding anyway,
Will bring you to the plateau of the human condition.

There may be times when you feel despondent about your fate,
And these times are needed to prevent us from becoming insensitive to others.
There are many more times when we are filled with the feeling of pride,
And these are the times that should be remembered and enjoyed.

November 2nd, 1993

Sharing the feelings and things that mean the most to you,
And caring for the ideas and feelings of someone else,
Is what is meant by marriage of two souls.
There can be no substitute for the warmth shared by two people so joined.

The miracle of finding someone with which to share yourself,
Is one of the wonders of the world, and should not be taken for granted.
So many never truly find the right person for life's journey,
That those of us that do should count our lucky stars and tell each other how lucky we are.

November 2nd, 1993
(Part B)

Leaving all thought of self behind us when beginning a relationship,
Is not so easy as we think should be the case.
It takes a lot of conscience effort to adjust the way we view life alone,
And what it means to be two instead of one.

The adjustments needed are a learning process for both,
And preconceptions about how it should be between you may sometimes hinder a relationship's progress.
For each person brings with them their own ideas as to the perfect relationship,
And sometimes the meshing of two sets of ideals does not go well.

When you have found another that shares most of your own thoughts as to a relationship,
And the differences between you are not insurmountable,
Then your new found pairing can bloom into a love that will have a better than average chance of lasting.
Keep in mind that both of you will have to nourish the seed for a healthy bloom.

November 2nd, 1993
(Part C)

The understanding necessary between two lovers,
Does not come magically simply because they profess their mutual love.
It requires a life time of experience and cultivation by all those associated with both parties,
And it also needs constant rekindling to nourish a long lasting relationship.

There are many variables in a relationship,
And if you have not solved the great majority of them between yourselves,
You will find rough going on the trail to happiness.
If you love is strong, you can overcome all obstacles life may put in your path.

November 2nd, 1993
(Part D)

Sometimes all that you do seems futile,
And nothing that should have a simple answer, does.
It is in these times that you should not look for method behind the madness,
But to some other aspect of your life altogether.

November 3rd, 1993

There are many aspects of life that may be temporarily beyond our comprehension,
And many of these will become clear with the passage of time.
Do not over concern yourself with what is now unclear,
For with a little persistence most things in life can be understood.

November 4th, 1993

Coming to the realization that not all in life will go your way,
And perhaps some things of real importance shall;
You will begin to understand what really counts in life,
And not be so involved in the more meaningless aspects of materiality.

Giving proper perspective to possessions,
Is a key step to true happiness,
And looking for something better than what we have,
Can lead to a life time of regrets instead of enjoying all we do have.

November 5th, 1993

Inspecting your life only to find that you feel something is lacking,
Can either make you take action to change or leave you bemoaning you plight.
Do not be of the latter type, for we can all use a little change,
So long as we do so for the better and not simply for the sake of change itself.

Wondering why so many are unhappy with themselves,
And discovering that it is only society's ideal which makes them think this way,
Brings us to the concept that the majority of us have put to much emphasis on the wrong aspects of the human condition.
We should not be a slave of what society as a majority seems to expect from us as individuals.

November 5th, 1993
(Part B)

Leaving behind your preconceptions of how you are supposed to be,
And exploring all the aspects of your abilities and character facets,
Will broaden your perspective of everyone you come into contact with.
It will also make you more understanding and sympathetic to others.

Travel life's byways with care of how you progress,
And try not to trod on the people you come into contact with.
There are many ways to succeed in life,
But none are worth harming others for.